PEARSON   ALWAYS LEARNING

Kristine Hansen
Edited by
Jill Larsen

Writing in the Social Sciences

Fourth Custom Edition

Taken from:
*A Rhetoric for the Social Sciences: A Guide to Academic and
Professional Communication*
by Kristine Hansen; Edited by Jill Larsen

Cover Art: Courtesy of Neubauwelt and PhotoDisc/Getty Images.

Taken from:

A Rhetoric for the Social Sciences: A Guide to Academic and Professional Communication
by Kristine Hansen; Edited by Jill Larsen
Copyright © 1998 by Pearson Education, Inc.
Published by Prentice Hall
Upper Saddle River, New Jersey 07458

This special edition published in cooperation with Pearson Learning Solutions.

Pearson Learning Solutions, 330 Hudson Street, New York, New York 10013
A Pearson Education Company
www.pearsoned.com

Printed in the United States of America

5   17

000200010272020717

NC

ISBN 10: 1-323-38876-1
ISBN 13: 978-1-323-38876-1

This book is affectionately dedicated,
for the third time,
to my students

CONTENTS

9 RESUMES 105

10 LETTERS AND MEMOS 113

11 BASIC PRINCIPLES OF DOCUMENT DESIGN 127

12 GRAPHICS 139

13 ORAL PRESENTATIONS   157

1

RHETORIC AND THE SOCIAL SCIENCES

CHAPTER OVERVIEW

After reading this chapter, you should be able to answer the following questions:

1. What is meant by rhetoric?
2. What is meant by social sciences?
3. What does it mean to say that knowledge is socially constructed?
4. In what sense do the social sciences involve rhetoric?
5. How can you as a social scientist use rhetoric persuasively and responsibly both as a professional and as a citizen of your nation and the world?

The title and subtitle of this book yoke two terms—*rhetoric* and *science*—that are generally believed to name things that are incompatible with each other. The word *rhetoric* is in many people's minds a name for "fancy talk," language that uses figures of speech or a flowery style to draw attention to itself. In other people's minds it might be a name for "empty talk" of the type politicians are frequently accused of using. In the view of still others, it is a synonym for "propaganda," deliberately slanted, misleading language that can result in various levels of harm—everything from voting for scoundrels to participating in genocide—when uncritical people believe what they're told. In all of these views, rhetoric is language that masks a lack of real substance in thinking or that distorts what is communicated, drawing attention away from the ideas by clothing them in beguiling dress. At best, rhetoric is thought to be language that attempts to persuade audiences by appealing more to their emotions than to their reasoning ability.

Science, on the other hand, is popularly believed to name both a kind of inquiry and its results; that is, science is a body of facts that have been produced by rigorously controlled methods. When properly carried out, these methods result in the discovery of objective truths. "Objective" means that the truths are independent of the subjective perception of those who discovered them. These facts are usually said to "speak for themselves"; they seem so obvious and logical that the language used to communicate them is also considered objective, neutral, transparent, free from bias or emotion. Thus, scientific language has long been held to be the opposite of rhetoric. In popular thought, rhetoric is meant to persuade, sometimes in an underhanded way, while science merely explains the way things are, with no hidden agendas.

What, then, can rhetoric have to do with science, particularly the social sciences? What can it possibly mean to call this book a rhetoric *for* the social sciences? To answer these questions, it's necessary to provide a more complete understanding of both rhetoric and the social sciences. These fields of study both have long and fascinating histories, too long to cover in detail here, but a brief summary will help to show how the two are compatible, indeed why it is helpful to think of writing in the social sciences as rhetorical. As you read the following, you will see that language—even supposedly neutral scientific language—can't escape being rhetorical. And the consequences of that for you, as a student majoring in the social sciences, are important, because as you will see, studying what makes up rhetoric will help you to be both a more skillful analyst of the rhetoric you read and hear and a more effective practitioner of it yourself.

WHAT IS RHETORIC?

Rhetoric has been defined many ways in its 2500-year-old history. Most of the definitions have been positive, unlike many contemporary understandings of the word. The word comes from the Greek *rhetorike*, the name for the art of oratory, or public speaking. The great philosopher Aristotle, who attempted to catalog so many other fields of learning, also wrote a systematic description of the art of rhetoric. He defined rhetoric as the art of "finding the available means of persuasion" in any situation. His book *Rhetoric* explains how to find and arrange ideas for a speech, how to appeal to various audiences, and how to choose the right style—in short, how to use language skillfully to express one's thoughts so as to win the confidence and assent of others. He recognized that such a powerful art could be used for unethical purposes, but he believed that in itself, the art of rhetoric is neither moral nor immoral. He thought that rhetoric used by a moral person to argue for good purposes would be inherently more persuasive and therefore superior to the rhetoric of an immoral person with evil ends in mind.

Isocrates, a contemporary of Aristotle, also believed that rhetoric should be used for virtuous aims. In the school he kept in Athens, Isocrates taught his students to be effective leaders in public affairs; he also attempted to teach them to be ethical by example and by challenging them to choose good and noble ways of making their arguments effective. Since ancient Athens was a true democracy in which each citizen was expected to participate personally, instead of by electing representatives, a knowledge of rhetoric was paramount for each citizen because making effective speeches was the way to influence the debates of the legislature and the judgments of the courts. (It should be noted here that participation in public life was limited to male citizens; women, slaves, and other non-citizens did not have this opportunity.) All other facets of education were intended to give young men a store of knowledge to draw on in their oratory.

The Roman rhetorician Quintilian extended Isocrates' ideas, declaring that the rhetorician should be a "good man, skilled in speaking." Quintilian laid a foundation for schooling the young in rhetoric and other fields of knowledge that lasted through the Renaissance in Western Europe. Although theories of rhetoric underwent some important changes during and after the Renaissance, the art and practice of rhetoric remained central to education in Europe and America until well into the nineteenth century, when the ideal of the citizen orator began to falter. Skill in oratory began to take a back seat then, as correctness in writing became the new goal in language arts instruction at the university.

If rhetoric was so respectable for centuries, how did it get the bad reputation that it now so often has? Actually, suspicions about rhetoric were voiced almost from the start, most prominently by Aristotle's teacher, Plato. He thought that the art of rhetoric in the hands of an unscrupulous person had the power to make bad ideas seem like good ones; he was also troubled that rhetoric could make merely probable ideas seem like undisputed truths (see *Gorgias*). Plato believed that one must know absolute truths before learning to use rhetoric so that one might never use the art to deceive, either intentionally or unintentionally (see *Phaedrus*). Plato's fears about rhetoric have been justified over the centuries by people such as Hitler, Stalin, Mao Tse Tung, or Senator Joseph McCarthy, who have deceived others through their cunning use of language. As a result, the reputation of rhetoric has always had its shady side. On the other hand, Aristotle's, Isocrates's, and Quintilian's faith in rhetoric as a potentially positive force has also been justified by people such as Abraham Lincoln, Sojourner Truth, Elizabeth Cady Stanton, Winston Churchill, Martin Luther King, Jr., and Pope John Paul II, who have used artfully composed language to inspire their followers in times of crisis and change to achieve goals they believed would make their worlds better.

Although most people would agree that rhetoric based on absolute truth is preferable to rhetoric based on probabilities, they would also have to admit that knowing the truth about everything before advocating a course of action seems hopelessly idealistic, if not impossible—an unaffordable luxury, especially in the face of urgent decisions that we must make collectively all the time. In our shared public life, we have to decide such things as how to vote, spend tax revenues, create and sustain schools and colleges, plan cities and transportation systems, interact with our environment, encourage and maintain healthy families, choose between arguments in a jury trial, help the poor, and deal with lawbreakers. We all respond to rhetoric as citizens of neighborhoods, cities, states, and nations, and we must often do so by the light of what we believe is probably true, rather than what we know for sure. Many of us also use rhetoric in the public sphere as we write letters to the editor, speak out at city council meetings, or urge others to vote for a candidate or an initiative. As a result, it is important to study rhetoric, both to understand how to analyze the rhetoric of others and how to practice the art ourselves.

Rhetoric will be defined in this book as *using words and other symbols skillfully to articulate and advocate your beliefs about something you assume to be true by addressing an audience whom you want to persuade to consider your beliefs, by choice and not coercion, and possibly to cooperate with you in achieving a shared goal.* Let's break that long, complex definition down into six parts:

(1) *Rhetoric is using words and other symbols skillfully to articulate . . .* The key words here are "skillfully," which means using communally accepted conventions of effective form, a pleasing style, and correctness in language; and "to articulate," which means to state what you believe in precise words and clear sentences, arranged in a logical and compelling sequence.

(2) *. . . and to advocate your beliefs . . .* The word "advocate" means that you actively argue for your beliefs, as an attorney argues for a client, using the kinds of logic, reasoning, examples, facts, evidence, statistics, or other data that you and your audience consider valid and trustworthy. But because human beings also have emotions which can be very powerful factors in how we make up our minds about an issue, an effective rhetorician will often advocate a case by appealing to emotions as well as reason. However, an ethical rhetorician will avoid doing so in a manipulative way. Ancient rhetoricians recognized that rhetoric included both appeals to reason (the Greeks called it *logos*) and to emotion *(pathos)*.

(3) *. . . about something you assume to be true . . .* This part of the definition allows for either certain or probable knowledge. The key point is that you are convinced something is true or so probable that you are willing to urge that others consider and possibly share your view. In order for that to happen, your own conviction must ring true to your audience. Your listeners or readers must perceive you as a credible and knowledgeable person with their best interests in mind, one who would not willfully mislead them. Your character, as conveyed in your rhetoric, becomes another type of appeal to the audience, in addition to reason and emotion. Presenting yourself as knowledgeable, credible, trustworthy, and well-intentioned is called the ethical appeal, from the Greek *ethos.*

(4) . . . *by addressing an audience whom you want to persuade* . . .
Rhetoric by its very nature is communal; its aim is to construct the broadest possible consensus, encompassing as many members of the addressed audience as possible. Consensus is likely to come about when the rhetor successfully appeals to the needs, values, beliefs, and assumptions of individual members of the audience.

(5) . . . *to consider your beliefs, by choice and not coercion* . . . By using threats, extortion, torture, or some other unethical means of exercising power, you might get others to say they agree with you and to cooperate with you, but you wouldn't be using rhetoric. Rhetoric is language or other symbols used to present a point of view to an audience that is free to choose whether or not to agree with you. The audience has an important role to play in any rhetorical situation: They have to judge not only the soundness and logic of the argument offered them but also the character of the speaker or writer. If their emotions have been appealed to, they must decide if such appeals are fair and well-meant.

(6) . . . *and possibly to cooperate with you in achieving a shared goal.*
Often, the purpose of rhetoric is simply to gain the audience's fair consideration of ideas, and, if possible, their intellectual assent. But it may also be used to go beyond assent, to persuade others to *act* upon their conviction—to vote a certain way, to join a movement, to volunteer for a cause, to make a change in their lives. The stronger and more persuasive your appeals, the more likely it is that people will act to join you in whatever efforts must be made to achieve a goal.

In this book I will maintain that the above definition of rhetoric applies not just to public discourse but to university disciplines as well, the social sciences in particular. Like cities, states, and nations, academic disciplines are communities too—but they are highly specialized ones that people enter by choice rather than by birth or naturalization. As teachers and students, as current and future professionals engaged in understanding the world and creating bodies of knowledge, we use various types of rhetoric all the time to present our claims of knowledge to one another and to urge their acceptance.

Just as founders of the United States agreed long ago to construct a new society on the premises that "all men are created equal" and that power is located ultimately in the people, so academic disciplines are based on assumptions that the members of each discipline accept as valid. Although the rhetoric used in American political life is often scorned, we must not forget that using the power of language to act on each other is our principal way of bringing about change in our society. The goal of most political rhetoric is to help citizens work toward building and maintaining a society that furthers a nation's founding principles—although it's clear that there is often disagreement about how to do that.

Similarly, the rhetoric used in academic disciplines allows members of those disciplines to create and maintain bodies of knowledge erected on their basic assumptions. But members of a discipline also use rhetoric to question, criticize, and revise assumptions, principles, and theories. No university discipline claims to be based on indisputable, absolute truths; in fact, the history of each field of academic study is replete with examples of how the field has changed its basic principles from time to time. Even though the assumptions of a discipline are provisional, they provide a basis for the research, writing, and talk that to a large extent make up the discipline. They enable something like a broad communal conversation to be carried on.

The specialized conversation of academic disciplines brings up another sense in which the word *rhetoric* is used. For centuries, the word has been used as the name for the book in which the art of rhetoric is laid out as an object of study and a guide for practice. Since this book will present practical advice for writing persuasively in the social sciences, it is in that sense a "rhetoric." This book, or rhetoric, will instruct you how to write like a social scientist by teaching you about the genres and styles regularly used in the social sciences. More importantly, it will show you how these genres and styles reflect how social scientists reason and carry out research.

WHAT ARE THE SOCIAL SCIENCES?

The social sciences are the fields of learning and research that concern themselves with human behavior, human relationships, and the social, cultural, economic, and political institutions that human beings have created. Considering their broad scope, the social sciences encompass many university disciplines and sub-disciplines. Although they might be named and grouped differently on various campuses, generally they include at least the following six disciplines: anthropology, economics, history, political science, psychology, and sociology. Yet other fields of study are commonly grouped with the social sciences because they also deal with human behavior and institutions. These include communications, education, family science, linguistics, geography, organizational behavior, demography, international relations, counseling, social work, and criminology.

Another way to identify the social sciences is to say what they are *not*. They are not the physical sciences, such as math, physics, or geology; they are not the biological sciences such as agronomy, botany, or zoology; and they are not the humanities and fine arts, such as literature, music, and theater. Yet even this negative definition is in some ways inadequate, as various social sciences might draw on one or more of these areas of learning. Most of the social sciences, for example, make use of mathematical and statistical procedures. Geographers must know something of geology, climatology, and cultural studies. Historians and archaeologists must often understand agronomy or botany to interpret practices or evidence from the past. Cultural anthropologists and sociologists are interested in the role that the humanities play in people's lives. Furthermore, there are cross-disciplinary fields, such as political geography, created when two social sciences intersect, or psychobiology, created when a social science field overlaps with a natural science. Perhaps it is best to focus on what all the social sciences have in common: They all aim to understand humans as individuals and as social beings, using empirical methods, in order to point the way toward solutions for personal and social problems, small and large, that confront us.

The social sciences are all relatively young as university disciplines, most of them having been established as separate fields of study and university departments in the late nineteenth or early twentieth century. This is not to say that prior to that time no one thought about human behavior, relationships, and institutions. But many of the questions that now preoccupy the social sciences were generally treated within the single discipline of philosophy (and they still are, though differently from how they are treated in the social sciences). Then in the seventeenth, eighteenth, and nineteenth centuries the natural sciences arose as powerful fields of study that investigated and explained the natural world with increasingly greater precision, yielding beneficial applications in such fields as medicine and industry. These achievements led some to think that a "science of man" or a "science of society" could also be established. They reasoned that, just as physicists and biologists could explain the laws of nature, and therefore predict and attempt to control the effects of natural processes, so the sciences of humans and society might uncover laws of individual and social behavior that would lead to developing better human beings and more just societies.

Some social scientists now believe that finding social and behavioral laws as consistent and reliable as the laws of nature is a utopian goal, since human beings and their interactions are often unpredictable, being influenced by more variables than one could possibly control. Nevertheless, all social scientists aim to develop the best tools and methods for understanding how individuals and groups think and behave so that they can state or predict with some accuracy the *probable* truth about whatever they might study—the causes of eating disorders, the reasons for voting behavior, the significance of head-hunting among the Ilongot people, the possible outcomes of an international trade alliance, why the sixteenth century was an age of exploration in Europe, why the Bay of Pigs invasion failed, or how to stem the tide of domestic abuse.

This emphasis on the probable, you will note, is consistent with the definition of rhetoric established earlier. If absolute certainty eludes social scientists—and most of them would admit that it does—they find themselves in the predicament that the philosopher Plato most feared in people's learning to use rhetoric. Social scientists have to make the case for what they have discovered based on what is probably true rather than what they know to be absolutely and objectively true. Is this situation as dangerous as Plato feared? If social scientists can't base their claims on absolute truth, will their writing be deceptive and therefore harmful?

The answer is, "It depends." It depends to a great extent on the assumptions that social scientists begin with. In the nineteenth century, there was a group of people who called themselves "scientists" and called their science "phrenology." They believed that they could determine intelligence and character traits from the shape of people's skulls. They developed instruments for measuring the parts of the skull, and they created elaborate, scientific-looking drawings of various skull types, with parts and attributes of each neatly labeled. For a time many people accepted the conclusions the phrenologists came to, which included that some races are inferior because their skulls tended to be formed differently from those of supposedly superior races. Most people today would consider phrenology a pseudo-science because when one examines its tenets and applications carefully, it becomes clear that one of its main purposes was to justify racial segregation and discrimination. This example shows that the assumptions of a group who call themselves scientists may be heavily influenced by political and ideological agendas that are somewhat hidden because the science presents itself as impartial and neutral.

The phrenology example shows there is some danger in proceeding from merely probable assumptions. Nevertheless, current theories of how knowledge is created and disseminated suggest that arguments based on probabilities may not pose a long-term danger, *provided* a scientific community's conversation is open and welcomes any responsible participant. According to these theories, intellectual communities that develop and ratify new claims of knowledge do so by examining, moderating, and even censoring excessive or potentially dangerous claims. These theories contend that knowledge is not so much discovered as it is socially constructed.

THE SOCIAL CONSTRUCTION OF KNOWLEDGE

We often say that knowledge is "discovered," as if it were like an uncharted island where a ship one day lands. After that, the fact of the island's existence and location is known, and the captain of the ship usually gets the credit for discovering it. But if we stop to think about it, the captain must credit the shipbuilders who provided a seaworthy ship, and he owes a debt to the map-makers and inventors of the navigational instruments that allowed him to chart a course across the ocean. Nor would he likely have succeeded in getting there alone, so he must credit the crew of the ship whose teamwork kept the ship sailing on course in all kinds of weather. Perhaps he even owes some thanks to unpredictable and seemingly random events, such as a storm that blew the ship off-course for a day or an argument with the ship's mate about what course to steer. Maybe one of these seemingly unrelated events actually contributed to the island's discovery.

The point of this analogy is that no one acts completely alone in establishing a new fact or idea. Knowledge has a powerful social dimension, both in the way it originates and in the way it is disseminated. Even if the ship captain had sailed alone, he would have been dependent on knowledge created earlier by others. More important, he wouldn't be able to establish his discovery of the island as a fact if all he had to offer as proof was his own word. Before the island's existence would be widely accepted as a fact, some kind of evidence would be required that others would find plausible. The captain's private knowledge would likely not count as a fact for anyone else until he could offer descriptions, pictures, artifacts, corroborating testimony, or other convincing evidence that he had made a discovery. Furthermore, he would have to submit his claim of new knowledge to be judged by standards that the community finds acceptable. The ship captain's claims must be persuasive to the audience to whom he makes them.

But this analogy brings up a few interesting observations. First, despite the help that enables the captain to make his claim, in a society that believes in intellectual property, he will generally get all or most of the credit for the discovery. Second, the discovery of an island is important only in a larger political system that values adventurous voyages into the unknown and finds it important to know the location of islands. In some political systems this discovery might be unimportant, particularly if there were no resources or inhabitants on the island to exploit. And third, if there were inhabitants on the island, what about their perspective? What seems a discovery from the captain's point of view might seem like an invasion to the inhabitants. The words "uncharted island" take on a different meaning when you ask, "Uncharted to whom?" Perhaps the island was included on other people's maps long before our hypothetical captain arrived. These points remind us that credit and rewards for knowledge often accrue to those who already have power and status; that what counts as the discovery of an important fact is also socially determined; and that there are ethical questions to be considered in the production of knowledge.

In the social sciences it is in some ways harder to establish convincing claims of knowledge than it is to prove the existence of islands. Islands have a concrete, physical reality that can be empirically demonstrated. Although social scientists also claim an empirical basis for their knowledge, the concepts they deal in are nevertheless usually abstract. The facts that social scientists discuss do not lie about in the physical world, like stones waiting to be stumbled over. They are not discovered in the sense that islands might be. Instead, they are created, constructed, or made. None of these words is meant to imply that there is a basic dishonesty in the facts, ideas, and theories of the social sciences—that they are somehow just fabricated out of thin air. There is a basis for social science concepts, but that basis often lies more in the social organization of the disciplines than in the physical reality of the surrounding world.

Saying this may make it sound like the social sciences are unconcerned with reality. On the contrary, they are very much concerned with reality, but these realities generally take the form of something like an economic trend, a cultural practice, an event in the past, a behavior, or an attitude. Because these realities are abstract, the social sciences must collectively negotiate their understanding and ways of perceiving and describing them—in effect, their ways of making knowledge. This collective negotiation results in the social production of knowledge. It will become clear how knowledge is socially produced as we consider the steps that all social sciences follow in creating and establishing claims of knowledge.

THE PROCESS OF KNOWLEDGE-MAKING STARTS WITH QUESTIONS

The social sciences, like the natural sciences, were organized to answer questions that are of general interest to practitioners of those sciences. Questions are the starting point for all of the social sciences' knowledge-making practices. As the social sciences have grown and developed, the initial questions that were asked have produced answers and theories that in turn have spawned new questions and refinement of the original theories. Thus, previous research affects present research, so much in fact, that a scientist planning to extend an established line of questioning, say on the relationship between parenting and personality, is expected to read all the previous literature on that question and to determine how the new questions relate to already established answers.

The boundaries of disciplines also direct the line of questioning. Most of the social sciences are concerned in some way with the institution of the family, but the questions a sociologist asks about the family might be very different from those an economist asks, which in turn are different from those a historian asks. As Ziman (1968) has noted, each field of science is like a corporate enterprise in which there are general overall goals and purposes, yet much specialization throughout the ranks and divisions of the enterprise. Each person spends his or her time and talents working with colleagues to create and maintain some part of the overall field. Although there may be some friction and disagreement—or sometimes even competition—within a particular field, there is usually general agreement about the overall goals because the research agendas of each science are largely shared by their members. In each field some questions will be considered not worth asking because they seem uninteresting, they appear to already have definitive answers, or it's believed there is no good way of answering them.

Because there is some social pressure to conform to established research agendas, maybe some originality is stifled or some potentially interesting avenues are left unexplored. However, the social influences on the defining of research questions do not necessarily mean that an individual must cease to think critically and independently or give up the freedom to choose *how* to think. There are still ways for independent thinkers to inquire into issues that others consider uninteresting, and such mavericks often ask unusual questions and make surprising claims that persuade others to join them in changing the direction of a field. At such a time, rhetoric becomes an important tool for them to use.

Answers Come from Observation

To answer the questions each social science deems important, individuals must somehow observe the reality that will produce an answer, whether that reality is a past event, a person's behavior, or a political trend. Here the word "observation" is used in the broadest possible sense, to include everything from examining documents to interviewing people to using scales to measure attitudes. But observation itself is also socially influenced in several ways. The reality that the social scientist observes must first be selected or defined as an object for investigation. Some part of reality must be focused on and marked off from other, related phenomena that surround it. Social scientists focus on a reality in the ways their disciplines have taught them to.

Yet even focusing carefully on something does not make it accessible to direct investigation. It is not possible to just "read off" the meaning of any particular object or event simply by looking at it, like reading the label on a can of beans. The phenomenon must be interpreted. This interpretation is socially conditioned because observers view reality from the perspective created by their education, their cultural conditioning, and their personal backgrounds. In addition, observation always takes place from a particular standpoint because an observer can't stand outside of a particular time or space and observe something "as it really is." The act of observing is already the act of interpreting. Also, the interpretation one arrives at will depend on the questions one asks to begin with and on the methods and instruments that one uses to observe with. Since these often come from the intellectual community one belongs to, observation is, like the questions the scientist begins with, also socially influenced.

Observation Relies on Methods and Instruments

Using methods and instruments with which to observe reality is the third common characteristic of the social sciences' knowledge-making practices. Methods are discipline-sanctioned procedures for answering the questions of interest in that particular discipline. But no method ever just dropped from the sky. All methods are human creations; each method has a history, with a definite beginning and many changes and refinements along the way. So important is method that when social scientists write papers, articles, and books about their findings, they include detailed descriptions of the methods they used. They know that their claims of knowledge will be judged in part by how carefully they followed the procedures and met the standards their field currently considers acceptable.

INTERPRETATIONS OF DATA BECOME CLAIMS OF KNOWLEDGE

Social scientists use methods to create data, find evidence, or otherwise come up with results that can be interpreted and related to existing knowledge. Although findings sometimes are ambiguous and don't point to any larger conclusions, interpretations of new evidence usually either support or contradict existing claims. In either case, the scientist's goal is to make valid and reliable statements. The validity of an interpretation is established by adequate evidence and sound reasoning about the evidence. Reliability is generally established through separate studies of the same phenomenon that reach similar conclusions, suggesting that the results will hold up over time. In order to make valid and reliable statements, social scientists go through the steps previously described, but they also subject their initial interpretations to careful scrutiny and criticism before disseminating them more widely. Scientists working to answer a particular question often communicate with their colleagues about their research throughout the whole investigation; in this way, they benefit from the advice and criticism of others even before they have written anything for others to read.

CLAIMS ARE DISSEMINATED FOR PEER REVIEW

When investigators have finished their research and have written a paper, an article, or other document, they do not print and disseminate their findings immediately. Most informally seek peer review by asking colleagues to read and criticize early drafts of the document they have written. Besides this informal peer review, each field has more formal ways of conducting peer review of new claims so that they will be as strong as possible before being submitted to the discipline at large. This formal kind of peer review generally takes place in at least two forums that are a part of every social science. In the first, a scientist might read a near-final draft of a paper or present a poster about his or her research at a professional conference or symposium. The questions and comments the audience poses might cause the scientist to rethink and revise some parts of his or her paper. In the second, the scientist sends a draft of a paper to a journal or publisher. The editor then sends the paper to two or more reviewers who read it carefully and recommend publication, revision, or rejection. Very few articles or books are published without some additional revision recommended by the reviewers. Because the reviewers have different backgrounds than the writer, they may have different perceptions of what the writer has observed. By taking the reviewers' positions and perceptions into account, the writer can revise to make the final draft stronger and more acceptable to other members of the field to whom the research is finally disseminated.

What does all of this mean for you? It means that learning to think like a social scientist is a process of socialization into your field's assumptions about what knowledge is and about how to ask the right questions. It is learning to follow methodological procedures and techniques, often using instruments that yield precise results. It is learning to interpret results and make claims that your scientific peers can examine and criticize. Your goal in this process is to do your work so well and present it so persuasively that peers will ratify your claims as valid and reliable. Claims so ratified attain the status of facts. Knowledge-making is a long process, and as you've seen, at every step it is a highly social one.

Because the processes for producing knowledge are social, the objectivity so often claimed by the social sciences is really a kind of *intersubjectivity*. That is, different persons, each with a different subjective consciousness, agree on the interpretation of particular observations. While the facts social scientists agree on don't usually have the same kind of physical status as islands, they are nonetheless true for the discipline that created them. The goal of any science is to achieve the widest possible intersubjective agreement about the facts. This social process of constructing knowledge protects a discipline—and society at large—from whatever dangers might come from the idiosyncratic claims of individuals who want to claim they have discovered some new fact, when in reality they may have some other agenda in mind, such as self-aggrandizement or spreading a bias.

HOW PERSUASION CREATES CHANGE IN SOCIAL SCIENCES

Because knowledge is socially constructed in the way just described, it is fairly "safe" from the claims of cranks and crackpots who might have a pseudo-scientific ax to grind. The social nature of scientific investigation and the peer review system are actually rather conservative elements in the process of knowledge creation, acting to censor unconventional interpretations and claims. On the one hand, this kind of conservatism is good, because it prevents the scientific journals from being clogged with just anything somebody might want to write. On the other hand, this conservatism may make science somewhat resistant and slow to change, even when legitimate scientists make worthwhile claims. Such resistance happens particularly when scientists challenge existing facts. Because many established scientists have invested their careers in building up a body of knowledge, they may sometimes let personal feelings get in the way of dispassionate review of new claims, especially when they can exercise power as a reviewer or editor. Change does occur, but it usually takes time and convincing new evidence, presented with great rhetorical skill, to change previous perceptions and interpretations.

While it is disturbing to think that strongly held personal views or desires to control knowledge, not objectivity and common sense, may sometimes get in the way of establishing claims of new knowledge, it is worth remembering that "objectivity" and "common sense" are often nothing more than the combined beliefs and assumptions of those who have had the power to control which claims were to be admitted to a discipline's body of knowledge. As one example, consider that all of the social sciences were initially developed by men; since women researchers and their assumptions and viewpoints were often excluded from knowledge-making processes in the not-so-distant past, many have argued that the social sciences have had a previously unacknowledged masculine bias. As more women have entered the social sciences, new focuses of research and new frameworks for interpretation have altered these fields somewhat and have generated some lively debates about the nature and status of knowledge. New interpretations and new claims of knowledge coming from a different generation of scientists always have to be negotiated through a rhetorical process that, if successful, enables the discipline to rethink some of its basic positions and then proceed from more acceptable, more valid, more widely held assumptions. As members of a field work through these negotiations, they, like anyone using rhetoric in public life, must remember to demonstrate good will, good faith, and patience in order to avoid the crippling outcomes of acrimony, fragmentation, and silence.

THE RHETORICAL SITUATION

This chapter opened with the claim that the words *rhetoric* and *social science* are compatible. It has focused mainly on demonstrating that social scientists, because of the interpretive nature of their research, need rhetorical skill to make their knowledge claims convincing to their audiences. The premise of this book is that speaking and writing in the social sciences is not simply a matter of packaging "objective" truths in "neutral" language. Because social scientists construct their claims from the methods of observation used in their fields, and because we perceive reality to some extent through socially constructed lenses, communication in the social sciences always has a persuasive dimension; i.e., it is rhetorical. But the rhetorical skill you wield as a social scientist should never be deceptive in the way Plato worried all rhetoric might be; instead, it should be true to the most rigorous standards of inquiry your discipline has formulated and to the highest standards of honesty and respect for others.

Your rhetoric should result from a considered balance and interaction among the various elements that together define any *rhetorical situation*. The rhetorical situation is any situation in which rhetoric is called for—and that includes a great many! An abstract way of thinking about the elements of any rhetorical situation is shown in Figure 1-1 (based on Jakobson 1960). This diagram shows that in any situation in which you use rhetoric, you must consider these six elements:

1. Rhetoric comes from a writer or speaker (called the addresser) who has a purpose in communicating with others. The purpose might be to inform, instruct, persuade, convince, entertain, delight, or otherwise express oneself. Being clear about your purpose is one of the keys for being successful as a rhetor. Just as important, your rhetoric will convey an impression of who you are, as you will create a persona, a role, or a voice in the way you construct your message.

2. Rhetoric is directed toward an audience of readers or listeners (or both, called the addressee). The audience might be large or small; it might be close by or remote in time or space. It might be composed of people who are very knowledgeable about the subject or people who know little about it. They might be well-disposed or ill-disposed toward the subject and its author, or they might be entirely indifferent. Analyzing the characteristics

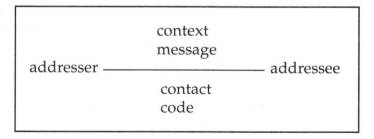

FIGURE 1-1. Jakobson's Model of the Rhetorical Situation

of your audience carefully before you begin to construct a message will enhance your chances of success.

3. Rhetoric is about a message you desire to send to the audience. This message might be about facts, ideas, feelings, impressions, or anything that one human attempts to convey to another through language. Often the hardest part of communication is deciding for yourself what the message is; the very act of attempting to put it into words may help you understand it more clearly and give you the opportunity to shape and re-shape it so that it includes all that you want it to.

4. The message is usually encoded in a natural language, but it might make use of other ways of symbolizing meanings, such as still or moving pictures, graphs, tables, statistics, mathematical equations, etc. Furthermore, the design of a printed message or the delivery of a spoken message is itself a part of the encoding of the message; they are not simply the packaging the message comes in, but part of the message itself.

5. In order for the encoded message to be conveyed to the audience, there must be a form of contact, a connecting medium. In a spoken communication, this medium is either the air conveying sound waves or electronic recording devices. For written messages, the medium might be printed or electronic. In our age, the computer has given us marvelous ways of combining almost all media, so that in a given message, you might see the author of the message, hear the author's voice, and read the author's words.

6. Finally, every communication occurs within a context; in other words, historical, social, cultural, ideological, and personal elements surrounding the communication impinge on the way it is constructed, conveyed, and received. That being the case, there is invariably a certain amount of "slippage" between the way a message might be intended and the way it might be understood. All messages are interpreted in ways influenced by the context, so various members of an audience might construe them somewhat differently. Knowing this, as a social scientist, you will want to take care to understand your audience and the context you share so that you can choose to use language and symbols that will be as unambiguous as possible.

You will note that the code is really the element that ties the other five elements together. This is significant because language, next to emotional bonds, is perhaps the strongest strand in the cord that connects us to others. To a great extent we know each other through the words we share. The way you use language as a writer is a way of conveying something about yourself to an audience who may never have met you. That is, through your writing you may reveal yourself to be educated, witty, friendly, aloof, or any one of many other possible descriptors. The language of much scientific writing doesn't allow for a lot of variation in the persona you can convey. In fact, one of the conventions of scientific writing is to convey the persona of a detached, thoughtful observer who doesn't let emotions get in the way.

The reality that writers aim to share with an audience is also mediated to us in great part by language. What you have learned already about your major discipline has come to you mainly through words that you have read or listened to. These words have shaped your understanding of the realities your discipline examines. As someone now learning to write in your discipline, you must express what you know about reality to your audience through language. You must choose language that is as true to your experiences and observations of reality as you can make it, and as clear to your audience as you can make it. (More will be said in Chapter 2 about how to analyze your audience and judge the best way to construct a message for them.)

Since social scientists deal with issues that affect us all intimately, it is important that you consider carefully who your audience is and how to communicate with not only your peers in the social sciences but with laypersons as well. As citizens we face serious problems in our families, neighborhoods, cities, and nation, and in a world community that is becoming ever more tightly knit through political and trade alliances and through advances in communication and transportation. Therefore, we need whatever expertise social scientists can offer to solve these problems that loom so large. Clear communication is an indispensable part of whatever solutions are offered. Because the members of different scientific communities often speak mostly to each other in their own discipline-specific language, there is a need for all of them to learn to use a more general rhetoric adapted to the ordinary citizen so that they can translate their specialized knowledge for the general public. (See Chapter 7 for guidelines on how to do this.) This book aims to help you acquire the rhetorical skill you will need to make a difference in the world, not only as a professional writing for your peers, but as a citizen who cares about the community you live in and who can apply your expertise to make it better. The centuries-old ideal of the citizen rhetor, espoused by Isocrates and Quintilian, might perhaps be revived if you and fellow social scientists learn to be skilled writers, capable of using the rhetoric not only of professional discourse but of public discourse as well.

REFERENCES

Aristotle. 1926. *Art of Rhetoric*. Translated by J. H. Freese. Cambridge, MA: Harvard University Press.

Isocrates. 1929. *Antidosis*. Translated by George Norlin. Cambridge, MA: Harvard University Press.

Jakobson, Roman. 1960. Linguistics and Poetics. In *Style in Language*, ed. Thomas Sebeok, 350–377. Cambridge, MA: MIT Press.

Plato. 1925. *Gorgias*. Translated by W. R. M. Lamb. Cambridge, MA: Harvard University Press.

Plato. 1914. *Phaedrus*. Translated by H. N. Fowler. Cambridge, MA: Harvard University Press.

Quintilian. 1921. *The* Institutio Oratoria *of Quintilian*. Translated by H. E. Butler. Cambridge, MA: Harvard University Press.

Ziman, John. 1968. *Public knowledge: An essay concerning the social dimension of science*. London: Cambridge University Press.

2

The Individual and Social Dimensions of Composing

Chapter Overview

After reading this chapter, you should be able to answer the following questions:

1. What is composing?
2. What are the general steps in the usual process of composing?
3. What are the individual dimensions of composing?
4. What are the social dimensions of composing? How does the notion of *genre* help both readers and writers?
5. What is involved in effective collaboration in research and writing?

Rhetoric of any kind seldom springs fully formed from anyone's mind. In order to be as effective as possible, rhetoric must first be composed. In ancient times, students often composed their speeches mentally because they lacked convenient and inexpensive ways to compose in writing. In modern times, however, most composing is done in writing. *Composing* is the name for the process of writing something—a term paper, a report, a letter, a review, or anything else—from start to finish. Actually, this "process" is really a set of subprocesses that interact with each other and recur in various ways depending on what you are writing about, whom you are writing for, what kind of text you are writing, and your own unique history and preferences as a writer. As you know, composing does not necessarily begin when you first set pen to paper or turn on the computer. Before that point you may engage in a process of thinking, discussing, listing, outlining, researching, gathering data, or otherwise generating ideas and facts to write about. Finding something to say, the first step in composing, was called *invention* by ancient rhetoricians.

Composing continues as you actually write a draft of your paper—that is, as you decide how best to organize the matter of your paper, how to structure paragraphs and sentences, and which words will best express your intentions. (The ancients called dealing with these matters *arrangement* and *style*.) Nor does composing end when you finish a draft. At that point, you often ask others to respond to your ideas and criticize how you've presented them. Then you revise to improve the content and organization of your paper. Finally you edit to make your paper stylistically correct and effective. Even after all of that, you may begin a new process of composing as you attempt to improve your first composition.

Some of these subprocesses of composing can run simultaneously: you can still be generating ideas and gathering information at the same time as you are drafting paragraphs and sentences. One subprocess can be interrupted for another to take place; you might pause in drafting, for instance, to revise and edit sentences and paragraphs already in place. Sometimes you may eliminate one of these composing subprocesses completely, out of choice or necessity; for example, when you write essay exams under time constraints you must do without outside criticism, revision, and editing.

Because of the various combinations and sequences of all the subprocesses that make up composing, it's safe to say that no two acts of composing are the same for two different individuals. They may not even be the same for one person writing two different documents. Because each act of composing and each person is unique, a textbook like this can offer only some observations that may help you reflect on how *you* write and decide whether your individual processes serve you well for all rhetorical situations. Setting aside individual differences, this chapter offers some generalizations and advice that may help you in your writing. You'll find here a brief discussion of the subprocesses of composing, followed by an analysis of both the individual and the social nature of composing. Because collaborative writing is an important feature of writing in many of the social sciences, the chapter ends with advice for working successfully with others to produce jointly composed papers.

THE SUBPROCESSES OF COMPOSING

COMMON WAYS OF PREWRITING

If you took a writing class in your first year at college, your teacher may have used the term *prewriting* to describe a number of activities that you can do to get your mind working on what to write about in a paper and how to organize it. You may have learned of some or all of these common prewriting techniques:

- Incubating
- Brainstorming
- Freewriting
- Questioning
- Discussing
- Clustering
- Outlining

Each of these prewriting techniques can help you get past "being stuck" because each helps you see that you *do* have something to write about. They help you get down on paper some of the thoughts that may be swarming through your mind. Simply getting your mind and your pen or computer cursor moving can help decrease the anxiety you may feel when you are assigned to write. You relax as you start thinking about the connections you can make between the ideas you've generated and captured in your prewriting. You start to see a main point you can argue for and the stance you can take in the paper.

SPECIALIZED KINDS OF PREWRITING

The above prewriting techniques are generally applicable to all forms and fields of writing. Other kinds of prewriting, however, are peculiar to academic writing, especially in the sciences. Though these are not always thought of as belonging to writing, they certainly belong to rhetorical invention—the process of finding something to write about. One such invention technique is keeping an *observation journal, log,* or *research notebook.* Another is using the *research methods* of the social sciences to create data to write about.

Observation journals, logs, and notebooks. The social sciences all depend on some form of observation and on careful recording of the data observed. For example, the historian must observe the previously unnoticed facts or the recurring patterns in the documents he reads in archives and libraries; he can't rely on only his memory to store all the information he discovers, so he keeps a research notebook, an organized card file, or computer files of notes. Similarly, the anthropologist pauses often to take careful field notes of customs and behaviors she observes in the people she lives among, not only noting their actions but also speculating on an interpretation. The psychologist doing repeated laboratory experiments with rats must keep accurate records of the behaviors he observes. The sociologist recording interviews supplements the recordings with notes about the context of each interview and facts about each respondent that she couldn't capture on the tape.

These methods of record-keeping may seem to be more removed from composing than the prewriting techniques described earlier, but they are no less important to successful composing. The social scientist may begin keeping a research journal or log with only a vague idea of what kind of text it will eventually grow into, but without the data recorded there, no paper of great value to other social scientists could be written. In most cases other social scientists expect that professional writing will be based on more than the thoughts in a writer's mind. This audience wants evidence that the observer was systematic and thorough in gathering, analyzing, and interpreting data that will support a claim. Without a research log or notebook to re-read, the social scientist would be less likely to find the themes and patterns that can be discovered in the daily entries. In that sense, some method of regularly recording observations is a kind of prewriting; without it, no findings could be established in a more formal document.

Research methods. In addition to keeping notebooks, logs, or journals, social scientists carry out systematic research using the specialized methods of their disciplines. Because these methods yield findings, evidence, or data that the scientist can then write about, they are also a highly structured form of prewriting. Certain methods have come to be associated with certain kinds of texts: participant observation with the genre called ethnography, experimentation with the experimental research report, observation of selected individuals with the case study. Chapters 3 and 4 discuss particular research methods in detail and illustrate the kinds of texts that result from several of these methods.

DRAFTING

Prewriting is usually followed by drafting. In this step of composing, you take the ideas or data you have invented and determine what interpretation you can support or what claim you can make. Often you state this interpretation or claim directly at the beginning of the draft, and this statement becomes the main point or thesis of your paper. In some kinds of writing, however, the interpretation comes last, as in the discussion section of an experimental research report.

Besides interpreting your data as you draft, you also organize it in a particular sequence, according to the needs of your audience and the type of text you are writing. You organize on two levels:

1. The macro level, i.e., deciding what large "chunks" of information should come before other chunks.
2. The micro level, i.e, what sentences should precede other sentences within paragraphs.

If you experience anxiety about writing, it helps when drafting to remind yourself that nothing has to be perfect the first time. A paper can go through several drafts—and usually should.

REVISING

Once you have a complete draft, the next step is usually to revise. To *re-vise* means to *re-see*. It means to pay attention to the overall structure of a text, considering again your sequencing of ideas, the proportions of space and emphasis you have given to particular points, and the amount of detail you have given in any particular part. When you revise, you do any or all of these three activities:

1. Rearrange
2. Add
3. Delete

A valuable way to revise a draft is to first set it aside for at least a day. Reading it again after you have rested and gained some emotional distance from your paper will help you to view it critically. Another way to evaluate your draft for revision is to let others read it. As they tell you how they viewed your draft, you may see its strengths and flaws more clearly so that you can capitalize on the strengths and eliminate the weaknesses.

EDITING

Theoretically, there is no limit to the number of times you could revise a single paper. Practically, however, there are limits, and the greatest of these is time. Few students have the time to revise a paper more than two or three times, as the term rolls on and other assignments must take precedence. Eventually a deadline comes and you must submit a final paper. But everyone should take the time to edit a paper before handing it in. Editing differs from revising in that it is local, rather than global. In other words, revising improves the macro-structure, and editing the micro-structure. It is usually best to wait until you have made large-scale, global revisions to your paper before you begin to edit. Otherwise, you might end up deleting something you've already spent time editing. After you get the structure the way you want it, you edit to polish the surface of your writing—making sure your sentences are clear and effective, choosing precise words, using appropriate grammar, and spelling and punctuating correctly.

COMPOSING WITH A COMPUTER

The computer has undoubtedly revolutionized most aspects of the writing process. While it may not make drafting any easier (especially if you don't type well), once you have an electronic draft, it is easier to revise because you don't have to retype every new draft. The blinking cursor allows you to add text at any point; the delete function lets you get rid of useless words and sentences with a keystroke; and the cut-and-paste functions permit you to rearrange sentences or whole sections of a paper without the scissors and tape of yesteryear. Spell-checkers make it easier to submit correct copy, and printer programs allow you to use typographical features that can improve the readability of your writing (see Chapter 11).

In some ways computers have made prewriting easier as well. Most libraries now give you access to huge databases, so searching for and retrieving information is more efficient than in the past. You can also use your computer like a research notebook, log, or journal to store bits of information that you can later retrieve and insert into a paper you are writing. The Internet can also make composing easier, as you can find some valuable information on the Web. However, it is an act of plagiarism simply to copy and paste text from the Web or use borrowed information without citing the source.

THE INDIVIDUAL NATURE OF COMPOSING

COMPOSING AS AN IDIOSYNCRATIC ACT

So far the subprocesses of composing have been portrayed as if they were the same for everyone. But they are not. In every act of composing, you can exercise some of your unique preferences and habits. For example, some people like to begin composing by sitting alone in the library or another quiet place with a favorite pen and a pad on which to list their thoughts. Others prefer the background noise of a cafeteria and perhaps a conversation to test their ideas, using a napkin or scrap of paper for jotting down good ideas. Still others have become so used to writing with a computer that they can hardly write with pen and paper anymore.

When some people start drafting, they like to work at a neat desk in the early morning, wearing a robe or comfortable sweats, with a favorite beverage beside them. Sometimes these writers have to get other important tasks, like cleaning the apartment, out of the way first so that they can concentrate on writing. Others write best late at night, with music in the background, oblivious to clutter in the room, dishes in the sink, and laundry piling up. Some people need three to four hours of uninterrupted writing time; others can write in twenty-minute snatches.

Some revise as they go, shaping sentences and paragraphs to their satisfaction, even correcting spelling and grammar before proceeding to the next part.

Others pour out words as they come, waiting until later to add, delete, rearrange, and edit. And all of us have our own prose style—a preference for certain words, a typical sentence length or construction, short or long paragraphs, few or many transitional elements. It's important to determine for yourself what times and places, what moods and physical states, what habits and rituals contribute to your productivity as a writer. It's also important to become conscious of style—both your own and others'—because the more aware you are of the stylistic options you have as a writer, the more control you have over shaping your meaning.

COMPOSING AS A PRIVATE ACT

Another sense in which composing is a highly individual act is that some writing is private. It isn't meant for others; it's just for you. You may keep a journal or a diary in which you record your thoughts about your life's experiences and your innermost thoughts and feelings. You may have the vague intention of someday letting family members or close friends read what you've written, but mostly the writing is for your own benefit. Even if you don't keep a journal, you may occasionally write as a way of helping you sort out complex matters— the pros and cons related to a particular decision you must make, for example, or as a way to blow off steam, such as a letter to someone with whom you've just had a heated argument (but which you probably won't mail). Perhaps you make lists that are just for you, of things to do, resolutions for improving your life, books you want to read. Maybe you are a closet poet, someone who loves to write poems or song lyrics you wouldn't dream of showing to others. And maybe you consider private the early writing you do for things that will eventually be read by others. Whatever your reasons for not sharing your writing with others, it's obvious that some pieces of writing are mainly for an audience of one—yourself—and the way you write them is nobody's business but yours.

But most writing is meant to "go public" eventually, and since it will then be read by others, there is automatically a social dimension to it. This social dimension will be explored next because it affects how you compose, particularly how you compose in the social sciences. The more you understand writing as a social transaction, the more successful you will be in participating in the intellectual communities of the social sciences.

THE SOCIAL NATURE OF COMPOSING

LANGUAGE AS A SOCIAL MEDIUM

Just as creating knowledge is a social endeavor (see Chapter 1), so the act of composing is permeated with the influence and the awareness of others.

Writing exists mainly for the purpose of communicating with others, after all, so it would be odd if it were not shaped by communal expectations and norms. Imagine how much more difficult writing and reading would be if there were no standardized spelling, no common agreements about how punctuation marks should be used, no grammar rules, or even conventional forms such as the business letter. Readers can understand writers more readily, writers can compose with greater confidence, editors can improve writing more surely, and typesetters can work more rapidly if there are norms and conventions that everyone understands and agrees on. Thus composing is social in the sense that the written language we use, with all its detailed conventions, is one that we share with others. Composing is social in other senses as well.

THE INFLUENCE OF AUDIENCES

The audience you write for exerts a powerful influence on what and how you write. Audiences can be divided into roughly two general classes: professional and lay audiences. If you have written for one of your professors about their area of expertise (and what student hasn't?), you have written for a professional audience. You know the pressure you feel to include accurate and complete information as well as to write about it in the way you think your professor expects you to—using the right terminology and the form of presentation that will most likely convince the professor that, even though you are a novice, you are beginning to understand the discipline and its norms for communication.

On the other hand, sometimes you are the expert in what you are writing about, and your audience is relatively uninformed about the subject—a lay audience. If you think carefully about how to succeed in communicating with them, you will realize that specialized jargon will not be appropriate, that you may have to use comparisons to familiar things to help them understand difficult concepts, and that the organization of your writing must be appealing and accessible to them. This is not to say that writing for a professional audience should not also be appealing and accessible; rather, it means that the level of language and the organizational conventions you might use would differ if you were planning to publish the same research findings in both a professional publication such as *Journal of Marriage and the Family* and in the popular periodical *Parents' Magazine*.

Audiences can vary widely. Depending on your subject matter and your purpose in writing, you will likely have to consider many of the following audience characteristics that may affect how you address them:

relationship to you	age
purposes for reading your writing	social class
familiarity with the subject	education
opinions and attitudes	religion

political affiliations	disability
geographic location	prejudices
race or ethnicity	gender

The level of complexity of your subject matter, the words you choose, the examples you use, and even how you organize what you write, should all be affected by your audience. The better you understand your audience, the more likely it is that you will make successful choices in writing documents that both inform and persuade your readers.

THE SOCIAL EVOLUTION AND INFLUENCE OF GENRES

Social influences are particularly important when it comes to the form and format of many documents. The social sciences, as noted in Chapter 1, function like highly selective and organized communities. As such they develop *genres*, forms of communication that provide socially constructed ways of dealing with rhetorical situations that occur again and again. For example, experimental psychologists have a recurring need to inform their peers about research they've conducted and to persuade their colleagues that these experiments add something important to the group's existing knowledge. Over the years, the genre of the experimental research report has evolved to the point that it now has seven very predictable features:

1. A title that explains directly and unambiguously what the article is about.
2. An abstract summarizing the basic aim, methods, and findings of the experiment.
3. An introduction that contextualizes the experiment in a review of related literature and states the research focus.
4. A description of the methods used to conduct the experiment.
5. A presentation of the results of the experiment, often including tables and figures.
6. A discussion of the significance of the results.
7. A list of references to articles and books cited in the report.

These various parts of the report are indicated by headings and typographical features (such as italics or boldface print) that help readers identify the parts quickly.

Beyond these standard parts, a typical style of writing is used in experimental reports, a style characterized not only by specialized vocabulary and preferred sentence structures but by the stance the writer takes toward the subject and the audience as well. A psychologist writing an article to publicize experimental findings would be wise to follow all of the above genre conventions.

They not only help readers rapidly locate the information most important to them, but they also show that the writer has internalized a way of thinking, researching, and writing that marks him or her as a member of the scientific community. Being able to use these features of the genre in the expected ways subtly influences the persuasiveness of the claim the writer is making.

Other fields have developed their own genres: case studies, position papers, narratives, ethnographies, and so on. In every discipline, each genre represents the result of an ongoing historical process of standardizing forms of discourse that enable the members of the discipline to establish and debate claims through journals and books. In a way, the members of a discipline carry on a conversation through their writing, and their genre conventions simply make that conversation more understandable to all. All genres are dynamic, however, not static, so every discipline is seeing changes in its forms of discourse, particularly as electronic forums such as e-mail, listservs, and electronic journals become more important as a medium for exchanging ideas.

The genres of each discipline reflect its assumptions about what knowledge is and how it is created: the methods of inquiry used, the kinds of evidence offered, and the presentation of the evidence show how the discipline's claims of truth are created and supported. But just as methods of inquiry shape genres, genres also shape methods. As one example, take anthropology. As it began to establish itself as a significant branch of inquiry, its main rhetorical genre, the ethnography, was shaped by the assumption that an outside observer, the anthropologist, could discover the important cultural practices of a given group of people (usually a "primitive tribe") through a process of neutral observation and then could report these practices in an authoritative manner, using "transparent" language (see Clifford 1986). A sort of imperialist assumption underlay this rhetorical practice: that the culturally superior anthropologist was able to determine and name the significance of the other culture's practices. In a sense, these early ethnographies intellectually "colonized" the natives' culture for consumption by interested readers, usually those back home in the anthropologist's native culture. This kind of genre had a powerful effect on new anthropologists entering the field, because as they read previous ethnographies of this sort, they took these as proper models for their own writing. In just this way, once it is established, a genre shapes future inquiry—until someone begins to question the values and assumptions the genre embodies.

That kind of questioning in the last two or three decades has led some anthropologists to write very different ethnographies from those that were written in the early twentieth century. Many recent ethnographies are characterized by their concern with the ethnographer's subjectivity; with the unavoidably interpretive nature of observation; with what can't be observed and therefore can't be interpreted and recounted; with the constructed nature of the stories the ethnographer tells; and with the role of metaphor, style, and other rhetorical devices used in writing the ethnography. In short, as anthropologists have become more aware of the rhetorical nature of their writing, their writing has become more self-aware and, many would say, more honest. Anthropologists have always tried to make true claims; now they seem to be more conscious that their claims to truth can only be partial and contingent. These changes in the genre of ethnography inevitably shape how the next generation of anthropologists will approach their own inquiry.

This interaction between methods of inquiry and rhetorical genres means that, as a would-be professional in your field, you would do well to learn to read and write as much as you can in your field's genres. But while reading widely in professional journals and imitating what you read may be an important first step, a lot of what you need to know and do will happen naturally as a matter of your being socialized into the field. Gradually, almost without your thinking about it, you will internalize your field's assumptions about knowledge and how it is created.

In that sense, learning to write for a *particular* social science discipline is a process that runs beyond the boundaries of this book or the time you may consciously devote to it in one course. All this book can do is teach you to examine how genres shape and are shaped by the kinds of inquiry your discipline is engaged in, so that you can be more conscious of how to compose its rhetoric successfully, and so that you can become more aware of the assumptions embodied in that rhetoric. These assumptions are not neutral; they reflect the values of the disciplines that created them. Sometimes these values and assumptions are (or perhaps should be) challenged and changed. Anyone who wants to change them, however, must first know the discipline's rhetoric well enough to mount an effective challenge.

THE INFLUENCE OF GENRES ON WRITERS

As you learn to write as a professional in your discipline, the particular subjects you write about and the genres you write in also construct you as a person. In other words, the genres of your field offer you a role to play, a persona to inhabit as you write, and a stance to take toward your audience and the material you are writing about. Even though you are an individual with a unique past and personality, your individuality has been constructed by the various social forces you have encountered in your life—your family, your peer group, your community, schools, church, clubs, teams, the mass media, and many other influences. In each of these networks of relationships with others and with the objects they are interested in, you have occupied a certain position that teaches you how the network uses language, prompting you to use it in certain ways, too. In joining a professional discipline, you enter into yet another network of relationships sustained in large part by the profession's rhetorical practices. You learn to occupy a position in that network and to use its language yourself to join in the conversation that maintains and furthers the discipline's projects. By becoming aware of how the rhetoric of your field constructs your thinking and your professional persona, you are more likely to control the rhetoric. That is, you will be able to speak the language consciously and by choice, rather than letting it "speak you."

COMPOSING COLLABORATIVELY

A final important way in which composing is a social act is that it may be done by more than one person. It is fairly common in some of the social sciences for researchers to work in teams—to collaborate. Perhaps some of your professors have assigned collaborative projects in courses you have taken. It is even more common for professionals outside the academy to collaborate on writing tasks, so it is worth understanding how to do it well, as there is a high possibility you will work and write with others at some point in your life.

Collaboration can lead to some important advantages: the division of labor, a high degree of individual specialization, collective reasoning and decision-making that may be superior to individual thinking, and increased efficiency, resulting in time and money savings. Collaboration also has the potential disadvantages of friction and disagreement among team members, some people not doing their share of the work, incompatibility in writing styles, and—especially for students—difficulty finding time to get together. But these disadvantages need not be part of collaboration if you enter into it understanding the different ways groups can function and if you plan ahead so that you can counteract possible problems.

Researchers (e.g., Ede and Lunsford 1990) who have studied various collaborative groups conclude there is a continuum of possible models with two extremes. At one extreme, the team divides all tasks completely; at the other, the team works together through all phases of the work. As an example of the first, imagine that four students are assigned to conduct an experiment to determine which of two kinds of peanut butter—one expensive and the other less so—students prefer in a blind taste test. They might divide the labor of running and "writing up" the experiment as follows: Anne goes to the library to find related literature that provides a context for the experiment, and she recruits participants for the experiment. Ben purchases the peanut butter and other materials, prepares the laboratory for the taste tests, and administers the samples to the participants. David is at the lab to record the results and then later analyzes the data. Carla leads the team and coordinates the whole process. After that, Anne writes the introduction to the paper and creates the list of references. Ben writes the methods section. David writes the results section, including the tables, and the discussion section. And Carla takes all the parts, blends them into one finished and edited report, then adds the abstract and title.

This example might be an efficient division of labor and use of time, particularly if each team member is doing the tasks for which he or she has a special talent, and if Carla successfully provides the leadership to ensure that the others carry out their roles well. But notice that the final paper might actually be stronger if the whole group, rather than just Carla, got together to join the parts and discuss the best ways of organizing paragraphs or phrasing sentences. Perhaps David, despite skill in creating tables, has overlooked something important that Ben could help him remember; maybe Anne will remember something from reading the previous literature that will strengthen the discussion. In other words, a complete division of labor throughout the whole process may not always result in the best product.

In the other extreme model of collaboration, all of the team members work together through all or nearly all phases of conducting the research and writing the report. This is roughly the model that was used by the four psychologists who wrote the influential book *Women's Ways of Knowing*, Mary Field Belenky, Blythe McVicker Clinchy, Nancy Rule Goldberger, and Jill Mattuck Tarule. For their research, they interviewed 135 women at length, using a set of questions that they had previously constructed together. Usually only one researcher was present at each interview, as the interviews lasted from two to five hours, and they took place in different geographical locations (so in this phase there was some division of labor). Each interview was tape recorded so that the whole team could listen to it. All of the interviews were transcribed, producing five thousand pages of text that each of the researchers read!

To analyze all of this data, the researchers together developed some categories for coding the respondents' statements along certain dimensions; then they read and re-read the transcripts, copying out quotations that illustrated various positions along these dimensions. The authors wrote independently but gathered as often as possible to discuss, to question, to rethink, and to rework each other's drafts. Over a period of five years, they shaped their study into a book. This kind of collaboration is obviously time-consuming, but it can also be very satisfying, especially if the group members enjoy working together and find a creative synergy in the give-and-take of lively discussion about ideas they all care deeply about. Despite the time and effort required, the results of this dialogic form of collaboration are often far superior to what one person working alone could create.

Obviously, there are many ways to combine the two extremes of collaborating: a team can divide some phases of the work of creating and writing a paper but work as a group on other phases. Regardless of how the process is managed, here are some important guidelines for student groups to follow in order to make the experience of collaborating more successful.[1]

[1] Adapted from Chapter 2 of *Learning Together: An Introduction to Collaborative Learning* by Tori Haring-Smith. Copyright © 1993 HarperCollins College Publishers. Used by permission of Addison-Wesley Educational Publishers, Inc.

GUIDELINES FOR WORKING IN GROUPS

1. **Keep the group small enough to succeed.** Since academic group projects usually require some meetings outside of class, your chances of coordinating individual schedules are greater if the group is small, usually not larger than four. Having more than three or four people in a group increases the difficulty of finding a time when all the group members are free to meet.

2. **Get acquainted as individuals and determine each other's strengths and weaknesses.** Whether you choose your team members or your teacher assigns you to work together, as a group you need to assess what talents you possess individually and collectively. Don't be shy about stating the special skills you possess: if you're a whiz in statistics, say so; if you can edit and proofread skillfully, everyone will be relieved to hear it. Each member should be equally forthright about any limitations that will affect his or her performance. For example, if you have a heavy course load and a part-time job, you should say so, as this will affect when the group can meet and the number or kinds of tasks you can be responsible for.

3. **Get organized.** It is almost always helpful to choose a leader, someone who will accept the responsibility of keeping the group on task and of monitoring each person's performance. Exchange phone numbers and e-mail addresses at this stage, too, so that you can contact each other when necessary.

4. **Lay the ground rules your group will abide by.** One such rule ought to concern how group meetings will be conducted so that each member will have relatively equal opportunities to speak. Another rule should address what you will do as a group if someone fails to do their assignments on time or adequately, or even fails to do them at all. If your instructor will have you evaluate each other at the end of the collaborative process, he or she will probably provide evaluation criteria. But as a group you can also determine fair standards that you will all apply equally in judging the quality of each other's contributions. Having rules and standards should help everyone proceed from the same assumptions and, later, make judgments about each member's performance, including what to do if someone doesn't do their part. If these prior agreements are in place, judgments are less likely to be taken as personal attacks and more as simply compliance with decisions the group made at the outset. For example, you might decide ahead of time if all group members do their assigned part well by the deadline that you will tell your teacher you all deserve the same grade. However, if someone's part is late, incomplete, or poorly done, the rest of the group will report to the teacher that the offender should receive a lower grade for their work (the severity of the penalty would be determined by agreement among the group members).

5. **Analyze the task you have designed or been assigned to do.** To analyze the task, ask questions such as these: Will you be conducting interviews, an experiment, or a survey? Will you be reading and analyzing documents? Will you be carrying out observations in natural settings? Will you be doing library research? How long will the eventual paper be? Has the teacher specified parts that it must have, or will you determine its organization completely? If you will determine the organization, spend some time thinking about what the eventual document might contain. Break the task into sub-tasks and discuss whether each should be accomplished by an individual, a pair of people, or more. Determine together a fair division of the labor, assigning tasks according to each person's particular abilities and limitations.

6. **Create a schedule for completing the sub-tasks.** Sometimes your teacher may impose a schedule for completing sub-tasks; other times, only a final deadline is given. If there is only a final deadline, set realistic intermediate deadlines that will help you monitor your progress and keep the work moving along at a steady rate. Remember that some delays are inevitable—a book you need will be checked out of the library, a group member may become sick and unable to finish an assignment, or a computer will crash. To help compensate for these setbacks, you can "pad" the schedule with a little extra time to allow you to meet the final deadline without too much stress.

7. **Hold regular meetings during the entire process to evaluate progress.** Your teacher may allow some class time for your group to work on its project, but even so you will probably need to meet at other times to keep the work moving along successfully. The group leader will need to be especially responsible to schedule meetings when all members can attend and to determine whether each person has completed their assignments. At these meetings you can share problems you have encountered and seek the advice of the others. You can also discuss what you have learned so far and begin developing the actual contents and form of the eventual paper.

8. **Draft, revise, and edit the paper as collaboratively as possible.** Once you have collected the data, found the evidence, or otherwise created what you will use in your paper, spend some time discussing as a group what it all means, and what the central arguments will be in your paper. Discuss and agree on how the paper should be organized. Then decide how you will create the first draft: Will you all get together around the computer at someone's apartment with plenty of pizza and soft drinks to keep you going? Will you work individually, each one taking responsibility for a different section? Will some of you work individually, while others work in pairs? Or will you find another solution?

   If you choose to work individually on different sections, arrange for everyone to bring or send computer files at the appointed time to merge the parts. After putting together a draft, send or print each member a copy and allow a day or two for everyone to review it and think about it. Then meet again to discuss how to revise it—what to cut, what to add, how to rearrange—and to focus on the details of editing—sentence structure, word choice, and punctuation. After agreeing on what the final draft should be like, assign one or more members to produce it, making sure that the best proofreader and editor in the group will be available to okay it before submission. Everyone should chip in to cover whatever costs are incurred—for high quality paper, laser printing, color graphics, and binding, for example.

9. **Evaluate the performance of your group and of individual members.** Your teacher may assign each of you to evaluate your group as a whole and each individual in it. In fact, if your teacher will grade your work, his or her evaluation will probably be affected by the way you grade each other. Even if no evaluation has been assigned, you may want to meet as a group one final time and consider how the process and the project might have been improved. This would be particularly important in a course in which your group will do more than one collaborative project. At the very least you should make some mental notes of what was successful and what was not so helpful so that you will be better prepared the next time you collaborate.

GUIDELINES FOR INDIVIDUALS

Besides the preceding advice for the entire group, here are some guidelines for you to follow as an individual so that you can contribute to the progress of any collaborative project you may be part of.

1. **Communicate with group members openly, honestly, and tactfully.** Your ideas are as important as anyone else's, so don't be shy about sharing them. If your other courses demand a lot of your time at the start of the project, you could offer to do more work at the end of the project to compensate. But don't promise to do what you can't possibly accomplish just to make a favorable impression. Tactfully express your concerns rather than attacking a team member's ideas or personality. Don't say bluntly, "That's a bad idea," but explain *why* you are concerned about the idea; for example, say, "That sounds like it will take more time than we have"; or phrase your concern as a question: "Do you think we have time to do all that?"

2. **Listen carefully to other group members.** Listening is more than just being quiet when others are talking. It is concentrating on what they are saying, watching their faces and body movements for clues to their meanings, their attitudes, and their feelings. Paraphrase what someone else has just said by asking, "Do you mean that . . . ?" Paraphrasing is especially important when you are not sure of the other's idea or when you think you may disagree.

3. **Learn and practice the art of negotiation.** Don't automatically shy away from conflicts. Conflicts can be productive if they are followed by negotia-

tion rather than a stalemate or a victory for one side and a defeat for the other. Negotiation resolves conflict by first finding the areas of agreement and disagreement and then by working towards a "win-win" solution acceptable to all. Negotiation requires patience, tact, and skill, as well as a willingness to compromise sometimes in order to help the group reach a consensus. Avoid being so attached to your own ideas that you won't even consider the other person's point of view. In fact, you should try advocating another person's position for a few minutes. This kind of empathetic role-playing can sometimes help you see the value of or at least the reasons for another person's point of view. By negotiating your way through conflicts, you and the other members of your group can all feel as if you "own" the solutions and the final product your group creates.

4. **Be a person whom others can count on.** Everyone's worst fear of collaboration (or worst experience with it) involves someone who is uncooperative or uncommunicative, someone unwilling to do their fair share, someone who agrees and then fails to do their assigned part, or someone who does such a poor job that the other group members feel penalized. Analyze yourself and your past performance in groups and determine if you have a tendency to be that kind of person. If so, it is likely high time to change some of your habits and make a more determined effort to be a team player. If you are someone who has had disastrous experiences working with others, who strongly prefers to work alone, or who has insurmountable difficulties in finding time to be part of a group, consult your teacher about the possibility of working alone or with people you already know and with whom you are likely to work well. Remember that the ability to work well with others is highly valued in the workplace and in graduate and professional schools, so to achieve your educational and career goals, there may not be a better time than now for you to learn how to be an effective collaborator.

AVOIDING PLAGIARISM AND GIVING CREDIT

In addition to full-scale collaborations, composing may have partially collaborative dimensions at any point. Even when you are not working on a jointly authored paper, for example, you would be wise to seek responses from others about your writing. One helpful strategy in prewriting is simply to discuss your ideas with others, such as a friend, a roommate, a mentor, or a tutor in your campus writing center. You can invite these same people to intervene in your composing process at the drafting, revising, and editing stages as well. It is particularly helpful to get a classmate's or tutor's response after you have a complete draft and before you begin to revise. Often, after spending hours on your writing, you are so involved in your ideas, and your paper seems so clear to you that you can't see its flaws. Or you know a part of your paper has problems, but you can't think how to fix them. A careful peer critic or tutor can offer you a reading that reveals where your paper doesn't communicate as well as you want it to. Your teacher may make this kind of review a mandatory part of composing your papers before you submit them for a grade.

In seeking feedback from others about your work, you are participating in a practice that is widespread in all professions. Virtually no professional in the social sciences or other fields publishes writing that hasn't been thoroughly reviewed by peers and then revised for improvement. There is a line to be observed, however, between acceptable and unethical use of others' help in your writing. You should ask others only for advice and instruction, not to do your work for you. As you probably know by now, using someone else's ideas or words without giving them credit is plagiarism. Buying an already written paper or hiring someone to write your papers is a serious breach of honesty that, if discovered, will result not only in academic and professional penalties but, more significantly, in your failure to learn and develop your own abilities to research and write.

You may certainly seek the help of others, however, as long as you accept the final responsibility for each phase of composing any paper you are assigned to write alone. If the form of the paper permits, you should graciously acknowledge the assistance others have given you—for example, in a preface, acknowledgments page, footnote, or letter of transmittal. If someone's contribution to your work turns out to be more significant than simply offering advice and instruction, if they provide you with data to use in your paper, for example, or if they actually write some parts of your paper, it may be more appropriate to consider listing them as a co-author. In all facets of collaborating with others—whether the collaboration is limited or full-scale—respecting others and attending to professional and ethical standards should be uppermost in your thoughts and actions.

REFERENCES

Belenky, Mary Field, Blythe McVicker Clinchy, Nancy Rule Goldberger, and Jill Mattuck Tarule. 1986. *Women's ways of knowing: The development of self, voice, and mind.* New York: Basic Books.

Clifford, James. 1986. Introduction: Partial truths. In *Writing culture: The poetics and politics of ethnography*, ed. James Clifford and George E. Marcus, 1–26. Berkeley: University of California Press.

Ede, Lisa, and Andrea Lunsford. 1990. *Singular texts/plural authors: Perspectives on collaborative writing.* Carbondale and Edwardsville, IL: Southern Illinois University Press.

Haring-Smith, Tori. 1993. *Learning together: An introduction to collaborative learning.* New York: HarperCollins.

Miller, Carolyn. 1984. Genre as social action. *Quarterly Journal of Speech* 70: 151–167.

3

RESEARCH METHODS, WRITING, AND ETHICS

CHAPTER OVERVIEW

After reading this chapter, you should be able to answer the following questions:

1. In what sense does writing begin with and extend throughout the research process rather than merely follow it?
2. What does it mean to say that methods are "disciplined inquiry"?
3. What is meant by quantitative methods? By qualitative methods? What are the pros and cons of each kind of inquiry?
4. What is an IRB and what is its function?
5. What are the ethical and legal requirements for involving human beings in research?
6. What is plagiarism? What is fraud? Why are these ethical lapses so serious and so detrimental to the scientific enterprise?

RESEARCHING IS PART OF WRITING

The documents that social scientists write are more likely to be persuasive when the scientists have used a method their readers find acceptable. If scientists do not follow the procedures and meet the standards that their colleagues find persuasive, it really won't matter how eloquently they write the final document about their research. Their rhetoric will not be persuasive if the evidence it is based on has been gathered sloppily or interpreted carelessly. Since good writing in the social sciences begins with finding or creating the evidence that will eventually be used in the document, using a research method is a kind of prewriting—yet a highly structured kind, much more rigorous and time-consuming than, say, freewriting or brainstorming.

If you will think of methods in this way, you should be more conscious throughout the research process of the paper you will write. You should begin thinking about the rhetorical situation for this paper even as you plan your research. For example, you should consider your audience from the first: What evidence will be sufficient to persuade them that your conclusions are reasonable and acceptable? What kinds of data will they expect in order to be convinced that your hypothesis was correct? The more you know about what your audience will require as sufficient proof, the more careful you will be as you plan your research, collect evidence or data, and consider plausible interpretations.

You should also be thinking about the genre of the paper you will be writing. What things are usually part of such a paper? A review of literature? Quotations from primary sources? Vivid descriptions? Detailed narratives? Tables and graphs? The results of statistical tests? A bibliography? The better you understand the genre conventions of the paper you will be writing, the more likely it is that you will gather all the information you will need to write it. Instead of thinking of research as something you do first and then "write up" later, you should think of writing as something you are doing all along as you research—from formulating your research hypothesis or question to choosing a method to collecting and interpreting data to proofreading your paper.

METHODS AS DISCIPLINED INQUIRY

A good definition of method would be simply "disciplined inquiry." This definition implies not only that the inquiry is focused and rigorous, but also that it is sanctioned by a discipline. In other words, it meets the discipline's assumptions about what knowledge is and its standards for judging claims of knowledge. The formalization of methods of inquiry is largely responsible for making the sciences what they are today. Although humans have probably always carried out the kinds of experiments that helped them learn how to preserve foods, dye fabrics, or make bricks, for example, it was only in the nineteenth century that the experimental method began to be considered a special form of inquiry that produces a special kind of knowledge called *science*. Before then, the word *science* could be applied to any field of study, including the arts, humanities, and theology; it simply meant *knowledge*. Now, however, we generally consider science a special kind of knowledge that has been created in an especially rigorous way so that its claims will have widespread and long-lasting validity.

When we realize that scientific methods are human inventions and, as such, are not necessarily perfect in revealing all that we would like to know, we start to see that the claims of science also may not be perfect. This does not stop the quest for rigor, however. Methods are constantly refined by repeated use and by the criticism of peers in the scientific community. In this way, scientific methods are always changing in the hope they will yield ever more reliable results. Experimental scientists have refined their method, for example, to remove as much doubt as possible from claims of knowledge by focusing on certain variables in the complex flux of events surrounding them. By controlling other variables and their own biases, experimental scientists attempt to manipulate the selected variables to establish cause-and-effect relationships, and then to state laws that can be used to predict future behavior. As a result of this remarkable endeavor to make experimental inquiry rigorous, the popular view of science is that it is knowledge produced by the experimental method.

However, the experimental method is not the only method of science, especially not the only one used by social scientists. Some social scientists long ago rejected the experiment as the one and only way of establishing valid claims of knowledge. The experiment is simply not appropriate to answer some kinds of questions. Also, because experiments focus on selected variables to study while controlling others, they create artificial situations unlike those that exist naturally. If the object of the social sciences is to describe human behavior, critics claim, then experiments may not be appropriate because, by their design, they may alter the very behavior that is of interest.

Some critics of the experimental method favor studying human behavior in natural, not controlled, settings; they reject the premise of control in favor of observing the multiplicity of factors that influence behavior. Like the experimentalists, their goal is also to question and to observe, to describe, and to generalize. But they have created other methods that will permit them to seek knowledge in the ways they consider most likely to produce meaningful findings. Each of the methods that social scientists have used in the twentieth century is rigorous in its own way, and each produces knowledge that may bear the label of *science* in the honorific sense. Each method has its strengths and its limitations; each is suited to answering some kinds of questions about reality and not others. Each method is reliable to the extent that it represents a discipline's consensus about the most rigorous way to investigate the questions that the discipline pursues. And if a method is followed carefully, the knowledge it produces will be considered valid.

QUANTITATIVE AND QUALITATIVE METHODS

Methods are usually divided into two categories: quantitative and qualitative. As their names imply, quantitative methods yield data that can be expressed numerically, and qualitative methods produce data that must be described by their qualities or distinguishing characteristics. Two methods that are often quantitative are experiments and surveys; two that are generally qualitative are interviews and observations.

But there may be some overlap between these two categories of methods. For example, a questionnaire might ask both multiple-choice and open-ended questions. The answers to the multiple choice questions can be counted and expressed as numbers; then other numerical operations can be performed on those numbers, yielding quantitative data. The answers to the open-ended questions, on the other hand, are qualitative data; they might have to be read several times to see what general patterns or themes emerge. Similarly, observation in natural settings is generally qualitative, with the observer attempting to record and describe what he or she observes. But the observer might also count certain repeated behaviors and then perform additional statistical operations on these data. So a written report of research might contain both quantitative and qualitative results.

Proponents of quantitative methods sometimes assume that these methods are superior because numbers are generally thought to be "hard" and factual, to have a solid and unambiguous meaning. It is often said that numerical data "speak for themselves" and require little or no interpretation the way the "soft" and more "messy" qualitative methods do. Adherents of qualitative methods, on the other hand, often think these methods are superior because of the rich data they produce. For them, the details and the subtle differences in the data are precisely what is most interesting, and they relish examining the data and using their interpretive powers to make sense of it. They might view quantitative methods as too superficial, arguing that, in fact, numbers tell us very little about *why* people act or think as they do; like qualitative data, numbers have to be interpreted in order to be meaningful. Despite these differences of opinion, both kinds of methods are valuable, and social scientists should be aware of the strengths and limitations of each in order to choose methods that are appropriate to answer the kinds of questions they want to ask.

A strength of quantitative methods is that they can be used with a large number of participants. If the participants in an experiment or the respondents to a survey are numerous enough and if they were randomly selected, therefore representative of the larger population from which they are drawn, then the results of the experiment or survey are said to be *generalizable*. That is, even without surveying or experimenting on the whole population, the results will presumably hold true for the whole population the sample represents. Another characteristic of quantitative methods that might be considered a strength or a limitation, depending on your viewpoint, is that experiments and surveys are usually designed and then pilot tested or repeated until all the "bugs" are worked out. With this kind of careful advance planning, surveys and experiments can yield very precise answers to highly focused questions. The data collected can often be quickly analyzed using computer software that will test relationships between any of the variables the researchers are investigating. The significant investment of time to plan and refine the study at the beginning is usually compensated for by speed in obtaining results.

Yet because they often require special equipment, computer time and expertise, or printing and mailing, experiments and surveys may sometimes cost more to conduct than many qualitative studies. Another limitation of quantitative methods stems from the way they transform data into numbers, particularly into means (numerical averages). The emphasis on the mean performance of a group effaces the individuality of the participants. Depth of description may thus be sacrificed to the desire to make broad generalizations.

In contrast, a notable strength of qualitative methods, such as interviews, observations, case studies, and analyses of documents, is that they allow researchers to describe in depth the individuals and circumstances they study. Although qualitative research is also carefully planned, it is not so precisely scripted that the researcher has no chance to pursue interesting questions that may arise during the investigation; qualitative methods offer much opportunity to branch, probe, and question. Rather than attempt to remove or minimize the researcher's subjectivity through rigorous control, qualitative methods actually foreground the subjectivity of the researcher as someone with an active, questioning mind, someone who makes informed decisions throughout the whole process of gathering and interpreting data.

Perhaps a drawback to qualitative research is that it is generally time-consuming to carry out well, so it usually includes fewer participants than surveys and experiments do. Although the texts that result from qualitative methods may contain many interesting observations and valid inferences, because they are typically based on observations of only a few participants, they are usually not considered generalizable to a larger population. Nevertheless, even with few participants, qualitative methods yield much data that must be laboriously recorded and transcribed, read and pondered, coded and categorized. Although qualitative research can often be done locally at little cost, it can also be expensive if it involves travel or special equipment.

It is good to be able to appreciate both qualitative and quantitative methods, for even though you may be inclined in your field to prefer certain methods over others, you will no doubt be influenced all your life by knowledge that is created by both kinds of methods. Understanding all methods, with their strengths and limitations, will help you to be a more critical reader of all kinds of research that you will encounter as a professional or as a citizen. Table 3-1 sums up the differences between quantitative and qualitative methods.

TABLE 3-1. A Comparison of Quantitative and Qualitative Methods

	Types	Advantages	Limitations
Quantitative Methods	Experiments Surveys	Possibility of large sample size Generalizability and breadth High degree of control	Loss of particularity Possibly high costs
Qualitative Methods	Interviews Observations Documents	Rich data Particularity and depth Large scope for interpretation	Low generalizability Overwhelming data Time consumption

ETHICAL CONSIDERATIONS IN DOING RESEARCH

USING HUMAN PARTICIPANTS

Since social scientists are interested in human behavior and human institutions, they must naturally study other human beings when they conduct their experiments, surveys, interviews, or observations. Yet human beings are not like the rocks, plants, or animals that a physical or natural scientist might study. A geologist can climb around on a pile of rocks chipping off pieces to take back to the laboratory anywhere it is legal to do so. An agronomist needn't obtain consent from two strains of corn before cross-breeding them. And a zoologist doesn't worry much about rats' right to privacy (although the zoologist is expected to treat the rats humanely).

Obviously, humans are capable of much more complex kinds of behavior than rocks, corn, and rats. They also have rights and needs that social scientists must respect in their research. In fact, to prevent abuses of human participants in research, laws have been enacted in the United States to prevent physical, social, emotional, mental, or other kinds of harm to any participants in a study and to protect their privacy. Interestingly enough, these laws stem from the Nuremberg trials, held in the aftermath of World War II, to try Nazi party officials and military officers for war crimes. Horrific experiments conducted by the Nazis on human beings had come to light, and it was discovered that people who were forced to participate in these experiments had not been informed of the purpose or the consequences of their participation. The Nuremberg Code of the late 1940s was formulated to prevent future abuses of this kind. The cornerstone of this ten-point code was informed consent by participants. In 1974, the United States developed its own federal policies outlining ethical treatment of human participants in research. In 1979, the Belmont Report, produced for the US Department of Health, Education, and Welfare, focused on three main ethical principles that researchers need to follow when human beings are involved. These are as follows:

- *Respect* for the dignity and autonomy of individuals requires that participants comprehend the nature of the research, give their informed consent, and participate voluntarily.
- *Beneficence* means the researchers do no foreseeable harm to participants and maximize possible benefits while minimizing any possible harm.
- *Justice* requires researchers to recruit participants so that benefits and burdens are distributed fairly across social groups, classes, etc.

INSTITUTIONAL REVIEW BOARDS

In order to insure that research would meet the standards of respect, beneficence, and justice, in the 1970s the US government issued regulations requiring all institutions that receive federal research funds to create and maintain committees that would oversee all research involving human participants. These committees are called Institutional Review Boards for the Protection of Human Subjects—or *IRBs* for short. By now, on all college campuses where any federal funds are used (and that includes campuses where students receive federal grants-in-aid), there is an IRB that is charged with reviewing and approving research with human participants to make sure that it complies with the laws. At Brigham Young University, the IRB is located in the Office of Research and Creative Activities (ORCA). If you decide to conduct research involving human participants, you must comply with applicable policies and procedures of BYU's IRB. Typically, the IRB will require that you submit a formal proposal to conduct research with human participants. The IRB's focus in reviewing your proposal will be mainly on the ethical and legal issues associated with the research project; however, its technical merits are important too, as no research should waste participants' time. You are under an ethical obligation to disclose everything you plan to do in your research and, once your proposal is approved, not to vary from your plan without seeking additional approval for the changes. Those who review your proposal will make sure that you meet four conditions for ethical social science research: confidentiality, informed consent, protection of vulnerable groups, and minimization of risk. (More information about how to fill out an IRB proposal will be given in Chapter 5.)

Confidentiality. First, you must ensure the *confidentiality of human participants.* How you do this depends on the methods you are using. On questionnaires, respondents generally are not asked to give their names, so their anonymity is easily preserved. However, researchers frequently ask respondents to give demographic information about themselves. Sometimes the researchers may know who gave certain answers, but they must ensure that others can't trace any answers to a specific person. Experiments and observations can also be conducted with little or no need to learn participants' names. If names seem necessary when investigators are writing the report of their research, they may use pseudonyms. Reports of interviews are more likely to require names, so the interviewer must determine whether the informants want the interviewer to use their real names or pseudonyms. If at all possible, a report of an interview that created an oral history should include the informant's real name, but only with his or her permission, of course. Interviews with public figures—elected officials or other people who hold a public trust— would also include real names. Interviews conducted for the purpose of identifying attitudes and behavior would more likely use pseudonyms, since *who* said something is not as important as *what* they said.

Informed Consent. Second, human participants involved in research must know enough about the purposes of the study to give their *informed consent* before they participate. If you conduct an experiment, you must create an informed consent document for each participant to read and sign. If you conduct surveys and interviews, you must inform participants of the purposes of the research so that they can choose whether or not to proceed; if they do proceed, they imply their consent by completing the survey or the interview. If you conduct unobtrusive observations of people going about their daily lives (e.g., counting how many people come to a complete stop at a stop sign) you are not required to obtain informed consent. However, if your observation somehow intrudes in a participant's life so that they are aware of it, you must obtain informed consent. Typical elements of informed consent are as follows:

1. Who is conducting the research
2. Purpose or objective of the research
3. How participants are selected
4. Procedures to be used and how long the research will take
5. What the known risks and benefits are
6. Participants' voluntary status and right to withdraw without penalty
7. Promise of confidentiality
8. Name and phone number of contact person for questions related to research. (Usually, the name and phone number of the professor supervising your research should be used for this.)
9. Name, address, and phone number of an IRB contact person for questions related to rights of participants. (At BYU, this is the current chair of the IRB.)
10. Implicit or explicit statement of consent that the participant agrees to; signatures are required for explicit consent.

Protection of Vulnerable Groups. Third, the laws also carefully regulate and insist on strict monitoring of research conducted with the following *vulnerable groups*:

- People who are ill or physically disabled
- People who are institutionalized, including people in hospitals, jails, and prisons
- People who are cognitively impaired
- People under 18 years of age (minors)
- Pregnant women, if the research is likely to do harm to the mother or her baby
- Members of minority groups, when the focus of the research is on their minority status
- People under your supervision or authority, e.g., students whom you teach

It is possible to study vulnerable groups, but the proposed research has to undergo a much more thorough review than research with other groups or individuals not designated as vulnerable.

Minimization of Risk. Fourth, you must be able to show that participants will face little to no risk of physical, social, emotional or other kinds of harm from participating in your research. The nature of the research and the level of risk each participant is exposed to is one factor that determines how carefully a research proposal is reviewed. At BYU, there are three levels of review: exempt, expedited, and full-board review. The differences between these are summarized in Table 3-2.

Note that exempt review does *not* mean that no review is required. It simply means that the research is such that it can be reviewed and approved quickly. Because of time and expertise constraints, students should usually plan research that can be reviewed at the exempt or expedited level. This means the research should involve minimal risk to participants. Experiments are the most

TABLE 3-2. Levels of IRB Review

Type of Review	Level of Risk	Number of Reviewers	Approximate Time Required for Review
Exempt	Minimal	1–2	3–4 days
Expedited	Minimal	2–3	2–3 weeks
Full Board	Minimal	5 or more	2-month minimum

likely to pose some emotional risk because they sometimes temporarily deceive participants. If the participants knew exactly what the investigators were trying to discover, then they might behave in a way that would alter the findings. By creating a ruse, the experimenters are better able to control how the participants act.

While some social scientists have argued that there should be no deception in research, others have maintained that temporary deception may be justified if the knowledge sought is important enough to justify the ruse. The general consensus is that researchers should not tell participants something that is untrue, but they may temporarily withhold some information regarding the aim of the study. If the participants in an experiment are given general, yet still accurate, information, and if participation in the study does not pose a risk of significant harm of any kind, an IRB would likely approve it as meeting ethical standards *provided* the researchers debrief the participants afterward to inform them fully of the purposes of the experiment. Without this debriefing, the participants may incur some psychological harm as a result of believing something about the experiment or about their own behavior that is not completely accurate.

RESEARCH THAT QUALIFIES FOR EXEMPT REVIEW

In order for research with human participants to qualify for exempt status it must meet the following criteria:

- It must be non-therapeutic. That is, it must not be designed to produce a diagnostic, preventive, or therapeutic benefit to the participants.
- The data must be recorded in such a way as to protect the identities of the participants.
- The research must not deal with sensitive or private aspects of the participants' behavior, such as sexual practices or illegal activities. At BYU, this could include inquiries about participants' violations of the Honor Code.
- The research must include no vulnerable populations. However, if you were to administer a questionnaire to 100 first-year students about how they like college life, and if there were in that group one or two pregnant women, and five or ten members of minority groups, your research could qualify as exempt so as long as the questions were not about their vulnerabilities.
- There must be no risk of criminal or civil liability to the investigator or to his or her sponsoring institution in the event that a participant's responses became known outside the boundaries of the research project itself.
- As a result of the preceding restriction about liability, plans for publication must be appropriate to your level of expertise and the nature of the

topic. Since you are a student taking a course at BYU, the university has an interest in making sure that any research you make public would not embarrass the institution or its sponsoring church. Therefore, your intent to publish findings in venues outside the classroom must be stated in the proposal so reviewers can judge how appropriate the research is for public knowledge.

Although all of the preceding may seem like a formidable list of restrictions on research, there is still ample opportunity for you to use various research methods to answer interesting questions and thereby gain valuable practice in researching and writing. As you read the next chapter, you will begin to think of questions that you can answer using social science methods. You will learn how to plan a research project. If you plan one that includes human participants, you will also need to prepare a proposal and seek approval before proceeding. The campus IRB has a set of instructions and forms for you to fill out as part of a proposal.

WHAT DOES NOT REQUIRE IRB REVIEW?

At this point, you may be thinking, "What can I do without IRB approval?" This is a question often asked, and there are some good answers. Provided the research does not involve vulnerable subjects, sensitive issues, and identification of participants, the following would not require review by the IRB:

1. Students observing, surveying, or interviewing classmates in the class where the research is assigned.
2. Interviews with professors on campus.
3. Interviews with elected officials or others who hold a public trust.

In addition, students are frequently assigned to do projects or papers based on their contacts with other people in service-learning projects, internships, and cooperative learning. These and other such assignments usually do not require IRB approval because these activities usually do not fall under the definition of "research." According to "Guidelines for Defining Public Health Research and Public Health Non-Research," issued by the Centers for Disease Control and Prevention in 1997, "research means a systematic investigation, including research development, testing and evaluation, designed to develop or contribute to generalizable knowledge." Working with your professor or advisor in service-learning or internship situations, you could measure projects and assignments against this definition to determine whether they require IRB review or not.

PLAGIARISM AND FRAUD

In addition to meeting legal and ethical standards that prevent abuse of human participants, researchers in the social sciences must meet other ethical standards common to all professions. Two of the most important are not plagiarizing and not reporting fraudulent research results.

Plagiarism. Social science research usually builds on previous research; in fact, most social science documents review previous studies that attempted to answer questions related to those of the present investigation. Usually, the previous research is presented in summary fashion. Occasionally, however, some studies are reviewed at more length, and it becomes necessary to paraphrase or quote parts of the original research. In such situations, you must be careful to observe all the accepted conventions of paraphrasing, quoting, and document-ing the previous research. You are not free to borrow someone's ideas or lan-guage without citing the author; if you do so, you are implying that you thought of those ideas and created those words yourself. While it may seem a trivial thing to borrow a few ideas or words without acknowledgment, it is a serious breach of professional integrity; and if it is discovered that you have plagia-rized, there are serious consequences, similar to those following from the dis-covery of fraud.

Fraud. Fraud in social science research is reporting data that are fabricated (not actually obtained through the application of a method) or data that have been altered somewhat in order to provide more clear-cut conclusions. Data might be altered by conveniently leaving out findings that are inconsistent with the hypothesis or by altering numbers in order to obtain a particular level of statistical significance. Some researchers may feel strong pressure to report data that is somewhat or even completely fraudulent, particularly if they have a lot at stake. For example, young researchers just beginning their careers may feel the need to publish as much as possible quickly, so they may cut corners to get results that are publishable; their promotion or grant funding may depend on successful research that finds its way to print quickly. Similarly, students wanting a good grade in a course or trying to complete a thesis for graduation may be tempted to "cook" the data a little to have a more impressive study.

THE CONSEQUENCES OF ETHICAL LAPSES

You should scrupulously avoid plagiarism and fraud in any degree. You may get away with either for a time, but if you plan to make your career as a researcher, you are foolish if you think you will never get caught. As Chapter 1 explained, the social sciences are communal and collaborative enterprises. As members of these fields work to create knowledge that will advance human understanding, each person depends on work that others have done. Each person owes a debt to earlier researchers who have established reliable knowledge and pointed the way to new research; this debt is acknowledged through proper citation of earlier work. Others in your field will have read much of the same research as you, and sooner or later they will realize when you have borrowed information without proper acknowledgment. Your failure to give credit where it is due will result in a weakening of the trust that makes a social enterprise like science possible.

Like plagiarism, fraudulent research weakens trust. Your peers will trust that whatever knowledge they borrow from you or others meets the highest professional standards of using methods and interpreting data. If your peers ignorantly attempt to base new research on earlier fraudulent work, it is like building a house on sand. Far from being small or one-time breaches of honesty, fraudulent studies can have a ripple effect throughout the whole research community. Perhaps this is why the social penalties are so severe when plagiarism and fraud are uncovered: these ethical lapses waste other people's time and often their money, therefore consuming their good will and slowing the progress of the whole community of researchers.

Social scientists whose plagiarism and fraud are discovered face not only the tarnishing of their reputations and the loss of their peers' respect, but also the loss of grant funding and sometimes their jobs as well. Students who plagiarize or commit fraud indicate to their professors that they are not ready to be trusted to enter into the community of professionals. Whatever your status, there is too much at stake to cut corners. It is far better to take the time to meet the ethical standards your field has established because they are there to protect everyone's best interests.

4

INTERPRETING DOCUMENTS

CHAPTER OVERVIEW

After reading this chapter, you should be able to answer the following questions:

1. In what ways is reading a kind of disciplined inquiry?
2. Do the facts ever speak for themselves? Do numbers?
3. What is a primary source? A secondary source?
4. What are the general steps in interpreting source documents?
5. What are the general steps in writing a paper based on source documents?

Reading and interpreting documents is the primary method of the historian, who could not write history without diaries, journals, letters, newspapers, magazines, immigration data, military records, parish registers, ships' passenger lists, and other documents from the past from which to cull facts and piece together an argument. But other social scientists may interpret documents as well. For example, political scientists concerned with theories of government, public policy, and social practices also read and interpret documents—constitutions, manifestos, court rulings, laws, census data, or the writings of Machiavelli, John Locke, Alexis de Tocqueville, and James Madison, among others.

Some psychiatrists or psychologists may collect and interpret the writings of clients in therapy. Sociologists also interpret documents that relate to social behavior, a kind of research that is often called *content analysis*. Archaeologists attempt to decipher ancient writings and drawings on papyrus, clay tablets, or canyon walls. Economists may interpret documents composed primarily of numbers, such as gains and losses on the stock exchange, budgets, or reports of the national debt and gross national product. Historians have also become more interested in statistical data, as they attempt to write about common people and their daily lives rather than only about presidents, kings, and generals and the events they participated in.

INTERPRETATIONS DEPEND ON PRIOR KNOWLEDGE AND ASSUMPTIONS

When they interpret documents according to the methodological standards of their disciplines, social scientists are, in effect, practicing a highly specialized kind of reading. Although reading may seem to be a very straightforward activity, one that you have been doing since you were a small child, when you examine what goes into reading like a historian, a political scientist, a psychologist, a sociologist, an economist, or an archaeologist, you start to see what a complex practice reading is. An ordinary citizen simply reading the daily newspaper draws (often unconsciously) on complex cultural knowledge in order to make sense of a story about strife in the Middle East, a description of famine or drought, or a report of the latest medical findings.

When social scientists read the documents of interest to them, they also draw on the assumptions, the accumulated knowledge, and the interpretive practices they have learned in their disciplines, not to mention their own personal backgrounds and experiences. They are able to discern relationships in and draw conclusions from documents that might mean little to the untrained reader. But even training in a particular discipline is no guarantee that all practitioners will see eye to eye on the meaning or relevance of a particular document. Within a discipline, two readers with different theoretical orientations may interpret the same text differently. For example, a historian with a Marxist orientation will read differently from a feminist historian.

Reading is not simply a process of decoding what a text says. If it were, there would be only one meaning for a given document. Yet, as we know, all kinds of documents, from poems and novels to wills and contracts to the U.S. Constitution, have been interpreted differently. Sometimes disputes about interpretation are settled in court, as in the case of wills and contracts. The meaning of various parts of the U.S. Constitution is also often disputed; frequently, the combined interpretation of just a handful of people determines the course of the nation, as in disputes that are resolved by a 5-4 vote of the U.S. Supreme Court. Occasionally, justices of that court have also reversed the decisions of earlier justices; for example, the 1954 *Brown v. Board of Education* ruling overturned an 1896 decision permitting racially segregated schools, thus demonstrating that interpretations may change with the times and the attitudes of the people. Sometimes competing readings of a document never are reconciled, as in the case of literary works. Several interpretations of *Huckleberry Finn* are possible, and one cannot be declared absolutely "right," although some interpretations will be more plausible and persuasive than others.

Different interpretations arise because we bring to our reading, just as we do to our observations of the world, our particular personal history, prior knowledge, theoretical positions, assumptions, biases, and expectations. This is not to say that we can make a document mean anything we want it to—we can't, for example, pretend that Lewis Carroll's poem "Jabberwocky" is a recipe for spaghetti sauce. (Well, we could, but we would not succeed in making anything edible from using it as such, and others might question our sanity.) Despite differences in readers, words do have relatively stable meanings and documents do bear a relationship to the worlds in which they were created and which they represent. Thus, part of reading sensitively involves understanding the context of a document and, if possible, the rhetorical situation that produced it. It helps to know who created the document, who the intended audience was, the purpose of the document, what it has reference to, and the words or other symbols used in it. The more we know about all these factors, the more our interpretation will be shaped by them—pushed in a certain direction. The more reasonable readers possess a similar understanding of a document's context, rhetorical situation, and its language or style, the more likely it is they will interpret it similarly.

STATISTICS MUST ALSO BE INTERPRETED

We often believe that numbers and statistics, unlike documents composed mainly of words, are easier to interpret because numbers are less ambiguous than words. It is true that numbers refer to the size or amount of something; therefore, given precise scales or procedures to follow, two different people asked to weigh, measure, or count the same thing should come up with the same number. Yet the resulting number in itself is often trivial; what the measurement signifies in relationship to other concerns still has to be established.

As an example of how numbers can be interpreted differently, consider Richard Herrnstein and Charles Murray's book *The Bell Curve* (1994), which examined many years of data collected from administering IQ tests to Americans of all races. One of their findings was that, as a group, African Americans have scored an average of 15 points lower on these tests than other racial groups. The authors interpreted this difference as principally due to the genetic inheritance of African Americans rather than to environmental factors. They then concluded that there is little point in spending tax revenues for social programs that attempt to improve education and job preparation for African Americans, because no matter how much was spent, social programs would not raise intelligence, something they viewed as largely inherited.

Other scholars agreed that the 15-point difference in average IQ scores exists, but they interpreted its significance very differently. They point out that a single factor—intelligence—cannot be the sole reason for the differences in test scores and therefore for differences in social and economic matters. A person's environment obviously influences his or her success in life but so do such things as character, personality, motivation, social skills, and common sense. Critics of Herrnstein and Murray noted that IQ tests are often culturally biased and fail to measure various forms of intelligence. They concluded that what the average difference shows, if it shows anything, is that our society should create better ways of educating all its members and preparing them for the labor market (see, for example, Gould 1994; Heckman 1995; Brace 1996). As this example shows, numbers and measurements may be very precise, but they are mute about their meaning in relationship to larger issues and questions. Statistical facts don't necessarily speak for themselves; someone must speak for them, interpreting their significance. Because of their beliefs, assumptions, experience, and training, different people often interpret the same statistic differently.

Although reading and interpreting words and statistics is a fundamental practice in all of the social sciences, it is difficult to generalize about how to do it. Much of what you should do when you interpret documents or other artifacts will depend on the questions you are trying to answer and the quickness of your own mind in identifying a bit of evidence as significant or in perceiving a pattern in a data set.

READING SOURCE DOCUMENTS

In interpreting source documents so that you can create your own new text, here are some steps to follow:

Define the question you are trying to answer and limit it to something you can investigate, given constraints of time, budget, location, and availability of sources. As a student you probably don't have the time and resources to spend on a major project such as analyzing census data from several countries, but you can still conduct interesting research in a limited time using resources available in local libraries, archives, and even your own home. For example, say you want to understand some very recent history: how the image of the computer has changed in mass media from a futuristic, science fiction type of invention to a tool that has today become a standard fixture in education, business, and industry, and most people's homes—in fact, something many people carry about with them each day. Suppose you have only about four weeks to research this topic, and you have no funding for travel, long distance calls, or acquiring documents, so your main source of materials to answer this question is your campus and local libraries. In this case, you would probably decide to limit your study to just a few magazines that span a time period you could identify as important for investigating this issue. You might phrase your research questions like this: "How have the covers and full-page ads of *Personal Computing* and *BYTE* magazines changed in the period from 1995 to 2015? What do the images on covers and in ads reveal about the changing conception and role of the computer in American culture?"

Locate suitable materials that preserve traces of the reality (primary documents) or that interpret the reality you are interested in (secondary sources). To begin to answer the above questions, you would check campus and local libraries to see if they have complete collections of the two magazines from the time period you want to review. You could also search library holdings to see what previous work, if any, has already been done on this or related topics. By reading any previous research on the general topic, you could avoid simply repeating an earlier study (though you may want to repeat it if you believe the method of the earlier study had flaws that you can avoid in your research). You could also connect what you learn to what other scholars have already established. This might help you to begin your research with some plausible guesses about what you'd find. Connecting your findings to earlier ones would also shape your paper so that it would contribute to building a body of integrated knowledge on your topic.

Determine the authenticity and reliability of the sources you locate. For historical topics, it's important to determine that the primary documents you are working with are authentic. Some historians have been embarrassed after basing their claims on documents that turned out to be forgeries. You must also determine that the secondary sources you've chosen are reliable, ones that meet high standards for scholarship. For the computer example, you would want to ask whether the magazines you have chosen to examine represent conceptions of the computer that are typical of the time period you are interested in. If you plan eventually to claim that these two magazines have documented an important shift in society's thinking about the computer, they shouldn't be obscure magazines but mainstream ones that contributed to the shaping of cultural images of the computer. You could check subscription records for the magazines to see how widely read they were, and you could compare them with one another and other computing magazines to see if they all have similar images in them.

Ask the journalist's questions as you read. These questions are *Who? What? Where? When? Why?* and *How?* With reference to our example of images of the computer, you might ask these questions about the images you are looking at: What images are depicted? How are the images created— mostly by words? Or by a combination of words and pictures? Are the pictures drawings, black and white photos, or color photos? What is emphasized? How much text is there in comparison to photos and drawings? What does the text focus on? Who seems to be the audience the covers and ads aim at? Computer hobbyists? Business people? Families? Can you discern a shift in audience from 1995 to 2015? When in the time period you're studying did the mass-produced personal computer appear? How did its appearance affect the images recorded? By asking and answering questions such as these, you will start to see patterns in the evidence and begin to draw inferences that will become a claim to argue for in your paper.

 Analyze systematically. Even limiting your examination to a 20-year period, you might not be able to look at all issues of the two magazines. But you could decide to look at every other issue, every fourth issue, or every tenth issue, so that you would be systematically sampling the available data. You should have some reasonable method of selecting and reading the data so that you won't later be accused of simply looking for what you hoped to find while ignoring possible contrary evidence. Full-page ads might appear in several places throughout a magazine, for example, but they are often in the first few pages. To guard against the charge of selecting full-page ads that support your emerging thesis, you might decide to study only the first full-page ad in each issue you examine.

Take notes about <u>what</u> you find and how you interpret it. You should write notes describing what you see, including specific issues and page numbers in your notes so that you can eventually construct the bibliography for your paper. You should also photocopy several representative images to illustrate the trends that you identify. You might even want to construct a table or another way of counting the prevalence of certain repeated images. You would also do well to begin stating tentative interpretations of what these changes in images imply about society's conception of the computer.

WRITING ABOUT SOURCE DOCUMENTS

When you have gathered sufficient evidence to begin writing, follow these steps:

1. OUTLINE A PLAUSIBLE ARGUMENT BY ASKING THE FOLLOWING QUESTIONS:

Who is your audience? Ask yourself questions such as these: Who will read your paper? What do they already know about this topic? Will they be difficult to persuade? What kind of evidence will be most convincing to them?

What claim will the evidence support? Which of the possible ways of interpreting the evidence seems most likely, most believable? State a tentative thesis, keeping in mind that you can alter it later if you feel your claim is too narrow, too broad, or skewed.

What evidence will best illustrate your claim? For the example used here, you will certainly want to describe the overall impression of the many images you looked at and probably include some photocopies that most strikingly illustrate those impressions. If you have come up with some categories of images that change over time, you might consider using a table or a graph to depict the changes. (See Chapter 11 for a discussion of how to place and refer to illustrations in your writing.) If you have used secondary sources, you must also decide what information you will quote, summarize or paraphrase from them. Remember to document any borrowed information.

What is the best way to organize the evidence to support the claim? A common way of organizing historical accounts is chronologically. But you could also organize by categories of images you've discovered, using some chronological organization within categories. You might also discern themes in the material you amass and organize your paper around them.

What documentation will you need? If you have used only primary sources, you would need at least a bibliography of the magazines and the particular issues that you used. If you have used quotations or reproduced images from your sources, you need to indicate with a footnote, endnote, or in-text reference where each borrowed item appeared originally. Any secondary sources used should also be cited in the bibliography.

2. DRAFT YOUR PAPER

Actually, you will probably be drafting as you answer the questions given above. Expect to change your mind several times about what to claim, what to include, and how to organize it. Draft and redraft the paper or parts of it as necessary until you have shaped it to reflect the most plausible claims you can make, given the evidence you have.

3. SEEK FEEDBACK

Once you have a complete draft that you are fairly satisfied with, ask someone whose judgment you trust to read it and respond to its overall effectiveness. Better yet, ask more than one person. Listen carefully to their comments, but don't feel compelled to follow everyone's advice. Let your draft sit a few days and re-read it yourself, critically. You will no doubt see ways to revise it.

4. Revise and Edit Your Paper

Using the responses of others and your own sense of what the paper still needs, rearrange elements of your paper, delete unnecessary or confusing parts, and add details, transitions, and documentation, to make your paper effective and correct.

SUGGESTIONS FOR RESEARCH AND WRITING

1. If your parents or some other family members have saved letters, perhaps from a courtship or a period of military service, obtain and read the letters, looking for one or more themes that you could develop in a paper. Use the letters as primary sources, quoting from them to support your interpretations. If appropriate, locate and use secondary sources that will help illuminate the time period in which the letters were written. Use appropriate citations and provide a bibliography for all your sources.

2. Often when states, communities, or colleges approach an important anniversary (the bicentennial of their founding, for example), they write a history of the time period just ended. If you live in a place where an important anniversary is about to be commemorated, see if you can contribute to writing its history. If someone is coordinating the history, you may be assigned to read and interpret documents that contribute to one part of the total history. On the other hand, if no one is in charge of writing a history, you might volunteer to pore over documents that have been saved and write a brief history of some part of an overall project

3. How has student life changed on your campus in the past 60 years? There is likely to be an archive of student newspapers and yearbooks on campus that you can explore to answer questions that are interesting to you about your parents' and grandparents' college days. Here are some possibilities: What were the important campus issues in the 1950s? How important were sports or the Greek system or queen contests in the 1960s? Have students become more politically aware over the last 20 years? Have students become more career-oriented since 1980?

4. Study magazine ads for a particular kind of product (e.g., alcohol, cigarettes, cars, or headache remedies) over a period of 20–30 years. Note how the ads change, if they do, to appeal to different needs or desires of the consumer. What can you infer about how the ad makers viewed consumers in a particular time period?

5. Television programs are a type of text. They begin as written documents, but the viewer watches a script enacted, rather than reading it. Watch

reruns of a particular TV program over a period of several weeks, say *Leave it to Beaver* or *Happy Days,* and study how one character is developed. From that character's words and actions, try to infer what viewers valued in the era when the program was current and popular. Another possibility would be to compare two programs that featured African Americans as the main characters, e.g., *The Fresh Prince of Bel Air* and *The Cosby Show.* How do the characters, the plots, and the values differ between these two shows?

6. Identify one of the oldest of the major journals in your field. Check your library to see if it has the earliest volumes of the journal; skim several early volumes to identify a main research topic then. Read carefully two or three articles that report investigations of that topic. What are the research questions or hypotheses? What methods are used? What are the findings and how are they interpreted? How does the state of knowledge at that time compare to the present understanding of that topic? What can you infer about how your discipline has changed?

REFERENCES

Brace, C. Loring. 1996. Review of *The bell curve: Intelligence and class structure in American life,* by Richard J. Herrnstein and Charles Murray. *Current Anthropology* 37 (February Supplement): S156–S161.

Gould, Stephen J. 1994. Curveball. *New Yorker.* 28 November, 139–149.

Heckman, James J. 1995. Lessons from *The bell curve. Journal of Political Economy* 103 (October): 1091–1120.

Herrnstein, Richard J., and Charles Murray. 1994. *The bell curve: Intelligence and class structure in American life.* New York: Free Press.

5

PROPOSALS AND PROSPECTUSES

CHAPTER OVERVIEW

After reading this chapter, you should be able to answer the following questions:

1. What is a proposal? What is a prospectus?
2. What are the required elements of an IRB (Institutional Review Board) proposal? Why does the IRB require each of these?
3. How does an ORCA proposal differ from an IRB proposal?
4. What are the typical elements of a prospectus?
5. How can a prospectus help you be more successful in completing a long research and writing project?

Planning ahead is crucial to success in any kind of venture, including writing. Sometimes your plans for completing a writing assignment are so brief and simple that you can work them out and store them all mentally. Other times, you may need to at least scribble a brief list or informal outline to remind yourself of the things you want to include in your paper and the order you want to follow. Sometimes your planning may extend to making a formal outline of what you intend to write; your professors may even require that you submit such an outline. The longer and more complex the writing task is, the less likely you are to be able to succeed with simple mental planning. In such cases, prior planning becomes especially important and sometimes very complex itself.

For example, if you have ever tried to write a fifteen-page library research paper just two days before it is due, you know that the best-laid mental plans can be frustrated: You find the books and articles you hoped to use are still checked out or they've simply disappeared from the library shelves. Or you discover that so few people have written on your chosen topic that you can't find enough information to write even five pages, let alone fifteen. Or, even if you have enough sources, you find at the eleventh hour that you are still struggling to understand them and to figure out how to integrate them into a focused, coherent paper. Or you realize at 2 a.m., when the library is closed, that you don't have all the information you need to write the bibliography for a paper that is due six hours later. Any number of other things could also go wrong. By systematically planning several weeks before the paper's due date, you could avoid most of these problems.

An excellent way of planning long, complex research and writing tasks is to write a proposal or prospectus. While these two words are often used interchangeably, a distinction will be made in this chapter. The word *proposal* will be used for research plans that primarily involve methods other than library research and for other kinds of formal written plans, such as bids and grant proposals. The word *prospectus* will be used for plans to write a paper based primarily on library research. Prospectuses contain mainly information that helps the reader imagine a finished written product—a research paper, a dissertation, a book. While proposals also typically promise an eventual written document, it is usually not described in much detail. With proposals, something else besides your plans for a document is usually at stake—money, permission to go ahead with a project, or an invitation to be included in a conference or a publication.

PROPOSALS

Proposals are a very common genre in the worlds of academe, business, and government. In academic professions, calls are routinely issued for people to propose conference presentations, articles for a special issue of a journal, chapters for a book, and other such opportunities to share knowledge and advance one's career. Corporations, philanthropic organizations, and government agencies that grant research funds also announce calls for proposals to compete for a share of the available money. In the business world, proposals may be sought for innovative solutions. Because funds and other resources are limited and must be used in the wisest way, the managers of a business want to be persuaded that the investment will be worthwhile before committing money, time, personnel or other resources to a project. In government, proposals often take the form of a competitive bid for a contract that will be let to the person or company submitting the best proposal to provide a product or service.

Even proposals that are not in competition with others must usually comply with various specifications or measure up to standards predetermined by those with power to approve the proposal. Therefore, proposals stress the researcher's qualifications and preparation to complete the proposed task. They frequently include information that allows the reviewers of the proposal to determine whether the researcher has the necessary expertise to accomplish the task. One way of judging expertise is to scrutinize the proposal author's description of the methods or procedures that will be followed. If the proposal is for a grant, it will include a detailed budget. Often, a proposal will present a reasonable timeline for completing the project.

Because proposals can be written for many diverse purposes and can take many different forms, it is not possible in this chapter to describe or illustrate all kinds of proposals. In the course of your education, your career, and your civic involvement, you may have to write many different kinds of proposals. Teachers and co-workers will be able to help you with some aspects of preparing individual proposals. Beyond that, the best things you can do are to ask a lot of questions about what the organization is looking for in the proposal and study other proposals that were successful in situations similar to yours.

AN ORCA PROPOSAL

At BYU every year, undergraduate students have the opportunity to apply for funds to conduct research projects. The proposals they submit are judged in the various colleges and schools by faculty members, and the funds are awarded to the top proposals by the ORCA office.

THE PROSPECTUS

Publishers typically ask for a prospectus, rather than a complete manuscript, when an author contacts them with an idea for a book. By writing a prospectus, authors are forced to be as clear as possible about their plans, distilling their ideas persuasively in a very few pages. After reading a prospectus (and often having it reviewed by others), publishers can determine whether a project is interesting and promising enough to encourage the author to complete the manuscript. Often, on the strength of a rhetorically effective prospectus, the publisher will offer the author a contract. Similarly, a prospectus for a long academic paper helps both the student writer and his or her instructor come to an agreement about the worth and feasibility of the student's plans. Rather than being offered a contract, however, a student either receives permission and encouragement to proceed with the planned paper or receives advice on how to strengthen or redirect the prospectus.

A prospectus is commonly required in graduate school for a master's thesis or doctoral dissertation. Its primary audience is a committee of professors who must approve the project before the student can proceed. The committee members are not likely to approve a project that is trivial or uninteresting, one that would merely plow over old ground, or one that would be too difficult or even impossible to complete. So the graduate student typically must persuade the committee that he or she has answered these questions:

- What is proposed?
- Why is it proposed? What contribution to knowledge will the student make?
- What will the finished work include?
- How, where, and when will the proposed work be accomplished?
- What qualifications are required to accomplish the proposed project?
- Are the necessary resources available?

PARTS OF THE PROSPECTUS

Exploring what is involved in answering the above questions will help you better understand what a typical prospectus contains.

What is proposed? You undertake a research project in order to answer a question or a set of related questions, solve a problem, or address an issue in a new way—perhaps because it has been addressed inadequately in the past or perhaps because there are new methods to be applied or new evidence to be examined. In a prospectus, then, you should state at the outset what the purpose of your research will be—what question, problem, or need your research will resolve. It is also helpful to locate the problem in a context, for example to show what historical, social, or individual issues it relates to. Providing this context will also help you establish a rationale.

At the time you write the prospectus, you may not know exactly what answer you will find to your question, what solution you might propose to a problem, or all the new information you might turn up about your topic. But you should know enough to state very clearly the aim and the scope of the research you want to undertake. For example, suppose a new therapy, validation therapy, has been created for helping elderly persons with dementia, and you wish to know more about it. After considering how little you know about it, you determine that some good questions to start with would be, "How does validation therapy differ from reality orientation, the standard therapy used in hospitals and residential care facilities? What are the merits of validation therapy? What evidence is there that it has been used successfully?" These questions already imply a scope for the paper—limits that will make it manageable because you will focus on answering these questions and not any of several related questions you could also answer.

Why is it proposed? Always intertwined with the *what* of any prospectus is the *why*. Explaining why it is important to research the topic you have chosen constitutes giving a rationale or justification for your project. Your reasons may be partly personal. Continuing the example above, you may have a grandparent who suffers from a form of dementia. Or you may have worked with such persons or plan to work with them in the future. You will no doubt be more interested in researching a topic that draws you personally, and that alone is a good justification.

But remember that you will be writing your paper for an audience too, so you should be able to come up with some more "public" reasons. What will help your readers believe that it is important to do this research? What other reasons justify the time and effort you will spend researching it? What will be the value to your audience and others of the knowledge you will collect and write about? You don't want your audience to read your prospectus and say, "So what?"

For the therapy project mentioned above, for example, you could justify your research by noting the widespread incidence of dementia among elderly people, its debilitating effects on them, and the difficulties that caregivers face in responding adequately to the confusion and disorientation that these patients experience. Perhaps the current therapy is based on faulty premises or it is unsatisfactory in the way it works for some patients. Any research that promises to shed some light on a vexing health issue should be welcome to most audiences because it is possible that many people or their loved ones may be affected by such problems.

The rationale of a prospectus doesn't have to be long, but it ought to be presented carefully. You want your project to be approved, so give some good reasons why it should be. Check with your instructor, however, to learn whether he or she deems it appropriate to bring up personal reasons in the rationale. No doubt all researchers have a personal interest in the research they conduct, but sometimes they do not expressly state their personal reasons in their justification for the research.

What will the finished work include? Your prospectus should give evidence that you have thought about the paper you will eventually write. Because you have already stated the question or the problem and rationale in the introduction of your prospectus, in this part you can show how you plan to present the answer or the solution that meets the need implied in the rationale. To write this part, ask yourself these questions:

- What overall thesis will you argue for?
- What parts will you divide your finished research into?
- What order will you put these parts in? What should come first, second, or third? Last?
- How much space will you devote to each part—how much emphasis will each receive?

In prospectuses for graduate theses, this part of the prospectus usually takes the form of a list of chapters and a summary of what each chapter will cover. In an undergraduate prospectus, a more suitable form might be a preliminary outline of the eventual paper. This outline is usually done in the traditional way, with Roman numerals and indented subheadings. But it could be less formal, in paragraph form, with sentences describing the subtopics you intend to address. Check with your instructor regarding the outline.

Obviously, to write this part of the prospectus you will have to locate at least some of the library sources you plan to use and become familiar with what is in them. It won't do to simply imagine what your eventual paper will contain, hoping that you will later find just the sources you need to fill in the projected parts. What if no such sources exist or they are difficult to get? By going to the library as you prepare your prospectus, you can determine if your project is even feasible and avoid a last-minute attempt to find useable, reliable sources. And by skimming several of your sources weeks before your paper is due, you will already have begun your research, eliminating the need for frantic, late-night reading.

As you can see, a prospectus demands that you "get serious" about your topic early enough to explore it meaningfully. By showing your reader how you have limited the scope and contents of your project, the overview of your proposed research adds greatly to the persuasiveness of your prospectus and enhances the possibility that your project will be approved.

How, where, and when will the work be accomplished? In addition to describing the eventual paper you will write, for many audiences you may need to describe the process you will go through to write it. This description can take the form of a task breakdown showing how and where you will conduct the research. This task breakdown can also include a timeline showing what phases of the work you will have completed by intermediate dates before the final deadline. Including a task breakdown in your prospectus can be very helpful if you plan to conduct complicated research, requiring you to travel to more than one library, for example, or to procure documents through interlibrary loan, or to interview an authority on your topic. Also, if you need to manage your time carefully because of other commitments, planning a reasonable schedule and then sticking to it can help you meet the ultimate deadline without panic. Here are some intermediate steps you could use to create a timeline that will help you finish your research project on time:

- Begin research
- Create preliminary bibliography
- Start notetaking
- End notetaking

- Write first draft of research paper
- Get feedback from peers, teacher, or others
- Write final draft of research paper

The task breakdown in your prospectus might be very brief if your research will be limited to simply reading in your campus library. Similarly, creating a timeline might be a perfunctory step if your instructor has already imposed intermediate deadlines. However, you should not underestimate the time that will be required to do good work, and you should make careful plans for fitting each step of the research process into your personal schedule.

What qualifications are required to accomplish the proposed project? In addition to showing that you can complete the work within the constraints of time and location, you may need to persuade your readers that you have the required background, expertise, and training to accomplish the goal of your research. This would be especially true if you were planning to supplement your library research, say, with some interviews or with statistical data that you would need to collect, analyze, and interpret. Briefly describing your education, your previous experience with your proposed methods, and your other qualifications for completing the task is sufficient for this part of a prospectus. In cases where no especially difficult or unusual research techniques are involved, however, your readers are likely to take for granted your ability to complete the project, and you won't need to demonstrate it.

Are the necessary resources available? Beyond time and expertise, research often requires materials, instruments, and sometimes money to be completed. In more elaborate prospectuses, you would have to make the case that these necessary resources are available. A library research paper, however, typically requires only access to documents. You can usually use library materials at no or very little cost, so the important point to argue in this part of your prospectus is that the documents you need are relevant to your purpose and available for your use. You should also demonstrate that they are reliable and useful.

Together with the part of your prospectus that outlines the eventual form and contents of your paper, this part is probably the most important in persuading your audience to approve your project. It usually takes the form of a review of literature—so named because it surveys and summarizes the sources (the "literature") you have already located and shows how they can help you accomplish your research goals.

One possible way to organize the review of literature is to follow the preliminary outline you have already created. For example, if you have planned a paper that has four main divisions, you could similarly divide your review into four parts and summarize the sources that will help you write each part of your proposed paper.

Since your research and reading will continue after the time you write and submit the prospectus, your readers do not expect the review of the literature to be extensive or detailed. In fact, it might be appropriate to indicate that you intend to read sources you haven't yet been able to check out from the library. Your goal in writing this part of your prospectus is to persuade your audience that you have made significant progress toward finding, reading, and organizing information that will eventually be a part of your final paper. It is usually not necessary at this point to quote or paraphrase your sources extensively; instead, you should summarize in a sentence or two the main points of the books and articles you've skimmed, explaining how they will contribute to your project.

Another part of the prospectus that shows available resources is a selected bibliography of works you have identified as relevant to your research. This selected bibliography is usually attached as a separate section at the end of the prospectus, and it should be labeled and formatted according to the documentation style used in your discipline. It should include documents you have reviewed in the prospectus as well as documents you still intend to review. If you are required to use a minimum number of sources, obviously your list should contain at least that many. If no minimum was specified, you ought to list as many sources as you can find that show real promise of contributing to your project, without padding the bibliography just to make it impressive.

Note that any readers of your prospectus will review your selected bibliography carefully to determine whether you have used sound criteria to select your sources. These criteria include the following:

- Are the sources relevant to the proposed purpose?
- Are the authors and publishers of the sources credible and scholarly?
- Are the publication dates of the sources appropriate? For some topics, recency of publication is vital; for other topics, older sources may be particularly relevant.
- Are the authors and sources sufficiently varied so that the biases of individual works are balanced by works with different assumptions and approaches?
- Have you included all potentially useful sources?
- If appropriate, does the list contain a variety of kinds of publications? For example, does it include journal articles, particularly in fields where articles are the primary medium for disseminating information?

As you can see, preparing a prospectus that has all these parts will carry you far along the road toward a finished research paper. Your final paper will be stronger because of the careful planning you will have to do to prepare the prospectus. By starting early and answering the questions outlined above, you will avoid the stress of trying to write your paper in a few rushed days. You might even experience the pleasure—and relief—of finishing your paper ahead of schedule.

ORGANIZATION OF THE PROSPECTUS

Although the parts of a prospectus described above don't vary much, how they are organized in a particular prospectus can vary a great deal, depending on the requirements of the professor or department you are writing for. In most cases, the purpose and rationale of the proposed research project comprise the introduction. After that you may be required to use prescribed headings and sub-headings in a specified order so that readers can check the completeness of the prospectus and read or reread parts as they desire. If you are required to follow an organizational plan, it is likely based on current genre conventions in your field. The organization below is suggested mainly for pedagogical reasons—to teach you one way of writing a prospectus that includes the necessary parts. Your instructor may ask you to modify this organizational scheme to meet other objectives he or she has for you. A complete prospectus can be divided into these four main sections:

1. *Purpose and Rationale.* In this section, you describe the general context of the problem, state the narrowly defined question, problem, or issue you propose to research, and justify its importance.

2. *Plan of Work.* In this section, you outline the thesis, organization, and contents of the eventual paper you will write; you provide your qualifications as a researcher (if required); and you outline the schedule you will follow, including how, where, and when you will accomplish the various phases of your research (if necessary).

3. *Review of Literature.* Finally, you summarize what you have learned from your research so far, showing how the sources you have read can help you achieve your purpose and fit into your plans for the eventual research paper.

4. *Selected Bibliography.* Attach to your prospectus a list of the works you have consulted so far and still intend to consult. Write this list according to the specifications of your field's documentation style. Label it appropriately (that is, the APA style and Turabian parenthetical reference style call it "References"; the Turabian note style calls it "Selected Bibliography.")

In addition to following this suggested organizational pattern, remember that the proposal is a formal document; therefore, you should take care to do the following as you compose it:

- *Make the tone formal to match that of the proposed paper.* The prospectus is not like a chatty letter to your teacher, so avoid writing in a casual tone.

- *Revise and edit your prospectus carefully.* Its purpose is to persuade your audience that you have the ability to conduct the proposed research and write the research paper, so you should demonstrate that you can write well.

- *Write the bibliographic citations in the correct format.* Getting the bibliographic citations right at this point will save you time as you prepare the final draft of your paper. If you are using the APA style or the Turabian reference list style, note that when you write the titles of books and articles within the *body* of the prospectus, the titles should be capitalized according to standard conventions, even though they are capitalized sentence style at the end in the list of references.

- *Follow principles of good document design when formatting your prospectus.* Use headings that correspond to the parts of a prospectus described here; or use other headings that your instructor may specify. Use letter-quality printing and a good grade of paper. The professional appearance of the prospectus should enhance its persuasiveness and indicate that you take pride in your work.

6

RESEARCH PAPERS

CHAPTER OVERVIEW

After reading this chapter, you should be able to answer the following questions:

1. What are three general types of research writing?
2. Why is it important to begin research with a well-defined question?
3. Why is outlining an invaluable aid in conducting research and drafting a research paper?
4. What are three ways of incorporating source material into your research paper?
5. What changes are you allowed to make to quotations, and how do you represent those changes in your writing?
6. What are some techniques for writing smooth transitions to make your paper coherent?

No doubt you have written a number of research papers by this point in your education. And no doubt you have noticed that each teacher who has assigned a research paper has had somewhat different purposes and requirements than other teachers as well as a different way of evaluating your work. Some teachers prescribe the topic and make your grade depend heavily on following precise instructions for process and formatting the final draft a certain way. Others are more laissez-faire about such matters, letting you choose the topic, valuing mainly the content and originality of your paper, and grading you more on your demonstration of significant learning. Your work has probably been made more difficult as you have attempted to discern exactly what your teachers expect. While it might seem desirable for all teachers to agree on processes, formats, and evaluation standards for academic research papers, it is not likely ever to happen. The research paper as an academic genre is more variable than it is as a professional genre in a particular field of inquiry simply because professors have their own notions of what an academic research paper should do and be. Likely they are influenced as well by the kind of research writing they do for their own field. Unfortunately, this chapter can't completely overcome that variability.

Even though a major aim of this book is to prepare you for writing in graduate school and/or the workplace, it is impossible to model all the genres of research writing that any student reading this book might need to know now or in the future. Also, because you are still an undergraduate, the research paper you will write in this course is more likely to be an instrument for instruction and practice than it is a new contribution to knowledge that could be published in a professional journal. So this chapter will emphasize fundamental principles that are likely to be true across disciplinary boundaries, thus preparing you broadly for many types of research writing in the academy, the workplace, or graduate school.

One such general principle is that a research paper is fundamentally an argument, not simply an exercise in finding and stringing together information from a certain number of sources your teacher has assigned you to locate and use. The process of creating an argument from research—whether in the library, on the Internet, or from empirical data—includes these steps: (1) identifying the type of research writing you are expected to do; (2) formulating a research question and finding information or creating data to answer it; (3) planning and building your argument through outlining the parts and recording borrowed information carefully and ethically; (4) drafting your paper; and (5) formatting the final draft. Each step in this process will be discussed below except step 2, as that is discussed exhaustively in Chapter 4. Other chapters in this book also complement what will be said here, and you will be referred to those chapters as appropriate.

IDENTIFYING TYPES OF RESEARCH WRITING

Research writing can be thought of as a continuum: At one end is writing based on information retrieved from libraries and the Internet and at the other is writing about data gathered through empirical methods. These are not mutually exclusive categories because nearly all empirical research papers include some information from library and Internet research, and sometimes papers based mainly on secondary sources may also include bits of information from primary sources, observations, interviews, and perhaps even casual surveys and experiments. But for clarity's sake, the following discussion will distinguish some of the characteristics of three types of writing that can be found in research papers: reviews of literature, argumentative source-based writing, and writing based on empirical data. All three kinds of writing can be said to advance answers in response to an initial question asked by the researcher.

Reviews of Literature

In the phrase "review of literature," the term "literature" does not refer to poetry and fiction but simply to whatever has been published on a given topic. A review of literature is a standard part of the introduction of almost every paper written to present new empirical data. It answers the question, "What is already known about this topic?" Writers review the existing literature for several reasons: A researcher investigating a given problem doesn't want to reinvent the wheel, so he or she would be foolish not to learn how others have already answered the same or similar questions. The researcher can learn from the successes and shortcomings of previous research how to conceptualize the problem and also how to improve the methods of the present investigation. Further, the researcher wants to understand the prevailing consensus, if there is one, about the question at issue. Above all, the researcher wants to learn what previous investigators have either neglected to study or studied incompletely because he or she has to define a space in the existing literature that the new research will fill. By reviewing or summarizing what all previous research has contributed to the problem, the researcher not only shows readers that the latest investigation is well-grounded conceptually and methodologically, but also that new research is needed to enlarge the boundaries of knowledge on the particular issue. Finally, the researcher can use the conclusions of previous research to interpret and/or bolster conclusions drawn from the results of his or her own study.

But a review of literature can be written for its own sake as well, not only as the rationale for new empirical inquiry. In this case, it is meant to be a comprehensive summary of what is known about an issue. The task of writing such a summary entails, first, a careful library search to turn up all relevant articles and books and perhaps a careful Internet search to locate reliable peer-reviewed information. Second, it calls for patient reading of the sources with a critical eye toward the strengths and weaknesses, the contradictions and similarities of the accumulated studies. In other words, a good review of literature should not be a hodge-podge list-style summary of all the information you have uncovered. Instead, it should have a well-defined organizational plan that reveals the size and contours of knowledge on the issue; the various parts of the review should be proportionate to the varying emphases given the issue over time. Such a review of literature may or may not lead readers to see the gap that new research could fill, but it could very well have a thesis or an overall conclusion that you draw from having read the research. Your teacher may assign you to write this type of review of literature in place of or in addition to another kind of research paper this semester.

SOURCE-BASED ARGUMENTS

Many professors want you to learn how to construct not just a summary, but an argument, from reading the literature on a given issue. An argumentative paper based on library sources is usually less comprehensive than a review of literature. It will also have more of an "edge" to it than a review of literature because you, as the writer, will set out to prove a claim that you believe and that you can support with textual evidence. This claim, or thesis, will be the answer to the question that you posed at the beginning of your research process. Although you may have hunches and hypotheses, you shouldn't enter into your research already knowing the answer. Finding the answer to your question does not mean that you are free to pick and choose your sources so that you include only those that favor a certain position and ignore those that work against it. As a would-be scholar, you must give a fair hearing to all sides of any controversial issue, so you also have to read as much literature as is reasonable, given constraints on your time and your paper's length. You need to analyze the logic or methods of each study you look at to determine if they are valid and reliable, and you need to evaluate the results and conclusions to determine if they are justified. Wherever good opposing arguments exist, you must acknowledge and explain them, but you may be able to refute them with better or equally good arguments in such a way as to lend support to your thesis. Or you can modify your thesis so that it is not as sweeping as it may have been before you encountered strong opposing arguments.

EMPIRICAL RESEARCH PAPERS

A research paper based largely on empirical data also makes an argument in answer to a question, but the strategies for making and supporting the claim are somewhat different. When you do empirical research, you must create, not simply find and synthesize, the knowledge that you will write about. You do this by selecting a method and then collecting data via that method. When your research process is complete, you have to make your argument out of the data you have and not the data you wish you had. You must analyze and interpret the data to determine what conclusions you can draw. When your empirical data are qualitative, you will often use them in much the same way that library and Internet sources are used to create an argumentative paper. That is, you might use descriptions of observations or quotations from interviews much like quotations or summaries from print or digital sources to support a point. Nearly always, you will turn to secondary sources from the library or Internet to help you interpret your findings or to bolster them with the evidence of previous research. When your empirical data are quantitative, you will usually represent them graphically in figures and/or tables. You probably will also apply statistical tests to raw data that reveal whether they are significant, i.e., due to real definable causes, not random variation or chance. Statistical proofs of significance become very important sources of persuasion in an empirical argument based on quantitative data.

PLANNING AND BUILDING YOUR ARGUMENT

A good argument based on library or empirical research is never the product of an "overnighter" or even a few days' work. The three student papers described above are the end result of a three-month long process the writers undertook to plan, research, draft, and revise their arguments. They began early in the semester to define the questions they wanted to answer. Then they each wrote a formal prospectus (see Chapter 5) in which they proposed and outlined the argument they wanted to make and also proved that they had the library sources and empirical data to provide the building blocks for their argument. After getting their teacher's approval to proceed, they began reading and taking notes in earnest; then they began drafting their papers. When they had a complete first draft, they each received peer feedback (see Chapter 8); then, using their peer critiques and their own judgment about how to improve their arguments, they revised their papers substantially before submitting them for a grade. Several different tasks are important in this process of planning and building an argument: outlining, recording information, and using sources ethically. Each of these tasks is defined and illustrated below.

OUTLINING

Very few people are capable of outlining the final draft of a paper at the very beginning of their writing process, but this does not mean that an outline isn't valuable from the start. You can certainly outline your first draft at the beginning. From skimming your sources in order to write a prospectus (see Chapter 5), you can learn enough to outline a rough vision of the finished project—enough to get you going. Having an outline as you begin work will help you conduct research and take notes in a more focused and organized way. Not having an outline to work with at the beginning would be like starting to build a home without a blueprint: You would be making up your house (or your paper) as you went along, not really sure of what to include or exclude or how to connect things. Having a blueprint doesn't mean that you can't add a window or a closet or move an interior wall as your house is being constructed, nor does it lock you into any way of decorating your home. Outlines and papers are even more changeable than blueprints and houses. As you proceed in your research, you can change your outline to match what you are finding; as you proceed in your writing, you can change your outline to match your sense of the best way to organize your argument.

Knowing the conventions of outlining can help you as you plan and carry out your work. The purpose of an outline is to show how different parts relate to each other and make up the whole. The principles underlying a good outline are these:

1. Division
2. Coordination
3. Subordination
4. Parallelism

If you learned outlining as a child in school, you know that the traditional way is to use Roman numerals, capital letters of the alphabet, Arabic numerals, and lower case letters in alternation to represent the relationships of parts, as illustrated in Figure 6-1.

The four principles underlying good outlines are evident at every level of the outline in Figure 6-1. The first principle, division, is evident in the fact that there are eleven different headings in the outline; the indentations in the headings indicate that the divisions occur at four different levels. Notice that at any given level, there are at least two divisions. When you divide, you must always divide into at least two parts; therefore, there can never be an *A* without a *B*, a *1* without a *2*, or an *a* without a *b*. The second principle, coordination, results from this principle of division. When you divide one part into at least two sub-parts, the results should be coordinate with each other; i.e., they should be equally important and receive about the same amount of space and emphasis in your paper. To use a simile, coordinate parts should be like twins or triplets—in the same family, each unique, but all equally important. The third principle, subordination, also results from the principle of division. When you divide a more general part into more specific parts, the more specific parts should be subordinate to the part they came from, i.e., at a deeper level of specification than the more abstract concept they follow. To use another simile, they should be like co-workers subordinate to the same supervisor.

The final principle of good outlining is parallelism, which is to be understood in two different ways. First, concepts at the same level within an outline, because they are coordinate, should be conceptually parallel—of the same type and roughly equal in importance. Second, the conceptual parallelism is made evident through grammatical parallelism. Below is a segment of an outline that lacks both kinds of parallelism:

II. Causes of the American Civil War

    A. Slavery

    B. Southern rebels fired on the US Army at Fort Sumter

FIGURE 6-1. Illustration of the traditional outline format

I. First Major Division
   A. First subdivision of Part I
   B. Second subdivision of Part I
      1. First subdivision of Part I-B
      2. Second subdivision of Part I-B
         a. First subdivision of Part I-B-2
         b. Second subdivision of Part I-B-2
II. Second Major Division
   A. First subdivision of Part II
   B. Second subdivision of Part II
   C. Third subdivision of Part II

As you can see, Part II-A is a very large and complex concept that is not conceptually parallel with Part II-B, which refers to a single event that precipitated the Civil War. The two parts are also not grammatically parallel, as "slavery" is a single noun, and "Southern rebels fired on the US Army at Fort Sumter" is a complete sentence.

Using the principles of outlining will help you as you work to impose a structure on the material you gather through your research. As your research and writing near an end, you will eventually stabilize your outline in its final form. Having a solid outline at the end of the process will be helpful because it will then be a simple matter to turn your outline into a table of contents for your paper and use the headings from your outline as headings in your paper. These structural elements will guide your reader in how to understand the overall organization of your paper and the relationships between different sections and ideas in your paper.

USING SOURCES ETHICALLY

Regardless of the recording methods you use and how you present what you borrow, you must be careful to avoid plagiarism and use your sources ethically and professionally.

Avoiding Plagiarism. To plagiarize means to use an author's words or ideas without acknowledging that you have borrowed them, implying that they are your own. The word plagiarize comes from the Latin for "kidnapping."

Metaphorically, the etymology is apt because, if you plagiarize, you are kidnapping someone's brain child—claiming to be the originator of something that someone else took the time and trouble to conceive, bring forth, and give their name to. The copyright laws regard plagiarism as the theft of intellectual property, similar to the stealing of real property, such as jewels or furnishings. Legal protection against plagiarism extends not only to written documents but also to sound and video recordings and computer software. There are not only legal penalties for plagiarism, but severe social and professional penalties as well. Occasionally the news media report on government officials, researchers, academics, and others in the public eye who have had past acts of plagiarism revealed, much to their embarrassment. Such revelations result not only in the loss of credibility and damaged reputation but sometimes in the loss of one's job. For students, the discovery of plagiarism is usually grounds for receiving a failing grade for the plagiarized paper and often for the course in which the plagiarism occurred. Extensive and repeated plagiarism may even be grounds for additional disciplinary action from the university.

But fear of repercussions should not be your primary motive for avoiding plagiarism. Your own integrity should motivate you to avoid this form of theft, just as your obligation to the communities you belong to should motivate you to respect the rules that make communal life possible. The temptation to plagiarize will be minimized if you remember that producing knowledge is a social, not solitary, endeavor. By carefully acknowledging what you have borrowed, you demonstrate that you recognize and are grateful for the contributions of earlier researchers. Far from indicating that you are unable to come up with your own ideas, when you document your use of others' ideas, you show that you are well-read in your field. By citing your sources, you also point the way for your readers to locate more information, should they desire to. Finally, a carefully documented paper shows the limits of your borrowing and makes your original contributions stand out more clearly against the ground of previous research that your ideas grow from. Your readers will be better able to recognize the extent and judge the value of your own thoughts as you carefully distinguish them from what you have borrowed.

Common Knowledge. There is one qualification of the rule against plagiarism: You are not required to cite a source for what is called "common knowledge." Determining what is common knowledge is often difficult, however, as it depends not only on who the writer is but who the audience is as well. The more educated and specialized both a writer and an audience are, the more likely it is that they can draw particular facts and figures from their store of knowledge without looking them up in other sources. Even though those facts originated with someone, after a period of time these ideas have become so commonplace that their origin is seldom mentioned. As you read your sources, you may see some facts mentioned with no source cited. If you see them mentioned repeatedly, you may assume that these are common knowledge for both the writer and the intended audience.

When you see specific facts mentioned without a citation, however, you should stop to ask yourself whether they are common knowledge for you and your intended audience. Ask yourself these questions: Did you already know these facts before you began your research? Is it likely that your audience already knows them? If so, you may include them in your paper without a citation. But if you find it necessary to take notes on particular facts, the very act of writing notes suggests that they were not common knowledge for you. You ought to cite at least the source where you first learned them, even if you can't cite the original source. When in doubt, it is safer to cite a source than to assume that something is common knowledge.

A Final Caution. As you take notes, you must be very careful with your sources as you are recording them so that you don't inadvertently plagiarize, misuse, or distort the information in your sources. You can also save time later when drafting by deciding how you would like to incorporate into your paper each item of information that you record. You have three options: (1) you can summarize, (2) you can paraphrase, and (3) you can quote. Each of these options will be explained in more detail and illustrated in the section entitled "Drafting Your Argument." Quoting your sources is not the best option because research papers are much more effective if you translate most of your sources into your own words and later recombine them in a way that allows you to make your own argument in a way that is both logically and stylistically coherent. Here are some rules of thumb to follow as you decide how to use a source at the time you make your notes:

1. Summarize lengthy and detailed information when you want only the main ideas or the essence of that information. Probably half or more of the borrowed information in your paper should be summarized.

2. Paraphrase information which you want to represent entirely in your paper but which you can say just as well in your words. Probably a third or less of the borrowed information in your paper should be paraphrased.

3. Quote information that you don't want to or can't summarize or paraphrase. Only about ten to fifteen percent of your paper should be quoted. You must write down quotes exactly as they are in the original source, so be very careful in transcribing or make photocopies to be sure you do not distort the original. To help you in choosing when to quote, here are some guidelines:

   • When the words of the original are open to several interpretations. For example, the First Amendment to the U.S. Constitution has been interpreted differently by various groups and at different times by the Supreme Court. If you were writing a paper about the disputes surrounding the First Amendment, it would be important to quote it rather than paraphrase it, since by paraphrasing you might inadvertently favor a particular interpretation.

- When the words of a document are the topic you are writing about. If you are writing about the language of a treaty, a trade agreement, a letter, a diary, or some other primary source, it is essential to quote actual excerpts from it, both to establish what is under discussion and to make your claims about it credible to the audience.

- When the words of the original are especially striking and a paraphrase or summary would diminish their impact. Occasionally, one of your sources will provide a phrase, sentence, or paragraph that is particularly well-said and memorable. If quoting it verbatim will add strength, insight, and color to your own argument, by all means quote it. But note that you can be selective about how much you choose to quote by paraphrasing or summarizing some of the original and using only those words that are particularly striking.

- When a quotation will help bolster the authority of the argument you are making. If you are writing about a controversial topic, trying to persuade a hostile audience, you and your argument may gain some credibility if you judiciously choose some quotations from respected sources that support your position. Be sure you don't distort the intentions of the original authors, however, by lifting supportive quotations out of their original context and using them in a way that the original author would find questionable.

DRAFTING YOUR ARGUMENT

Using your outline as the framework and your notes as the material to fill in and enclose the frame, you can begin to draft your paper. You may find it helpful first to turn your outline into headings for your paper. Every Roman numeral division of your outline will become a primary heading; every *A* or *B* division will become a secondary heading; and every *1* or *2* division will become a tertiary heading. (These three levels of headings are illustrated in Chapter 11, so no more will be said here.) Then, if you have handwritten or photocopied notes, sort your notes into piles that correspond to the divisions of your paper. If you have typed your notes in computer files, organize them so that they are easily retrievable to insert into the different parts of your paper. Now you can begin to write paragraphs under each heading that build each part of your argument, and you can incorporate your borrowed information into the paragraphs as needed to support the assertions you are making. You don't necessarily have to start writing at the beginning of your outline, though most people do. If you have a bit of writer's block about what to say first, start in the middle. Often, writing other parts of your paper will help you see more clearly what you need to say at the beginning to set up your main points and the conclusion.

As you are drafting, you will use your borrowed information as explained earlier, in one of three forms: summary, paraphrase, or quotation. Each of these is explained and illustrated next, followed by advice about writing transitions, introductions, and conclusions.

SUMMARIZING

To summarize is to distill the original source down to its essence, by capturing the main points and ignoring the details. A summary is therefore much shorter than the original. It is also written in your own words, though it might include a few quoted words for which you can find no synonyms or which you can't adequately express in your own style. Although you write a summary in your own words and style, you still must attribute the ideas to the author from whom you borrowed them.

PARAPHRASING

To paraphrase is to restate the original in your own words and syntax, while still capturing the entire meaning of the original. A paraphrase is thus about the same length as the original, and it parallels the original by following the same order and giving the same emphasis to ideas as the original. A paraphrase might contain a few quoted words or phrases you can't find appropriate synonyms for. When you paraphrase, you do not distort the intent of the original by leaving out ideas or by enlarging minor points or downplaying major points. The value of paraphrasing is that you can give your paper a more coherent voice and point of view by putting source information in your own words. But you still must attribute what you have borrowed to the original author, either as you introduce the paraphrase or in a parenthetical reference.

QUOTING

When you were younger, you may have "written" research papers by simply finding and quoting the exact words of many different writers. But now you know that quoting is the type of borrowing you should do least. An exception to this rule would occur when you are writing an empirical research paper based on interviews. Papers that consist mainly of many quotations strung together with a few transitional sentences tell your reader that you have failed to digest your sources well enough to present the information in your own voice and as support for your unique thesis. But that is only a part of what you need to know about quoting sources. There are many intricate facets to the mechanics of quoting, so how to do it according to accepted conventions is discussed and illustrated next.

FORMATTING THE FINAL DRAFT

Once you have revised your paper sufficiently that you are prepared to submit it, it is time to add the formatting your teacher requires. Formatting guidelines are admittedly arbitrary. Understanding that surface format features can and will change as you write for different audiences and purposes should help prepare you to be flexible about such matters in the future.

Following are typical elements for a student research paper. These elements correspond to those you would be required to have in an honors thesis or senior thesis at BYU.

1. *Title Page.* Because your paper is a final document, it should have a title page. The minimum elements for a title page are, of course, your title and your name. Your instructor may also want you to list the name of the course, the teacher's name, and the date the paper was finished or submitted.

2. *Table of Contents.* The table of contents, as previously noted, is the hierarchical arrangement of the headings used in the paper, with indentations showing whether each heading is primary, secondary, or tertiary. Following each heading is the page number where the reader can find the section of the paper under each heading. On the table of contents, it is helpful to use dot leaders, a row of dots running from the heading to the page number, as these help the reader's eye move across the page to the right number.

3. *Other Prefatory Pages.* If your paper contains any tables or figures, there should be an additional page following the table of contents entitled "List of Figures and Tables," or simply "List of Figures" or "List of Tables" if you have only one kind of graphic in your paper. The abstract follows these pages, and is headed with the word "Abstract." (For more information on using figures and tables, see Chapter 12; for more on how to write an abstract, see Chapter 8.)

4. *Pagination.* All of the above prefatory pages except the title page are numbered with lower case Roman numerals. The title page is considered to be page i; however, it is not numbered. The table of contents is numbered as ii, with other prefatory pages following in numerical succession. The first page of text is numbered with the Arabic number 1, and other pages are numbered successively. The list of references begins on a new page after the conclusion of the paper and is numbered with Arabic numbers succeeding the last page of text.

5. *Appendixes.* If you have one or more appendixes, they follow the list of references and are paginated with Arabic numbers succeeding the list of references.

6. *Double spacing.* Double space the final draft that you submit to your teacher.

CONCLUSION

As you come to the end of this long and detailed chapter, you are probably feeling a bit daunted by all you have to remember and to do as you write your paper. It would be impossible to take all of the steps outlined here in one short burst of work. Writing a strong research paper is a task that must be spread over many weeks if it is to be successful. At the beginning of the semester, the assignment to write a research paper can loom ahead of you like a grueling hike up a tall mountain. But rather than regard the assignment as an enormous obstacle in the path of your comfort and happiness, try to view it as an adventure and an opportunity to learn new and interesting things at each step along the trail. Choose a topic to research that genuinely interests you and set a goal to write a paper that will benefit you and others. Don't procrastinate starting to read, take notes, and write a rough draft. Divide your journey into stages and mark with satisfaction your progress to each milepost along the way. Then when you finally reach the summit by completing your final draft, you can look back with pride on your achievement and savor the view from the heights of your new knowledge.

7

PUBLIC POSITION PAPERS
AND OPINION PIECES

CHAPTER OVERVIEW

After reading this chapter, you should be able to answer the following questions:

1. What are position papers and opinion pieces? Who are they written for?
2. What are the steps in researching and writing a position paper or opinion piece?
3. How do the organization and style of position papers and opinion pieces usually differ from reports written for professors or for professional peers?
4. What would it take for a position paper or opinion piece to have an impact on public policy-making?

As a student of the social sciences, you are learning about social and cultural institutions such as governments, the justice system, schools, hospitals, churches, charitable organizations, youth groups, and families. In general, these institutions aim to promote a just, harmonious society and the development of productive, healthy individuals. It's probably clear to you by now, however, that these and other institutions are not always successful in reaching these goals. After more than 200 years of government under the United States Constitution, for example, there is still not complete harmony and equity among various groups in the USA. Some well-intended government programs and policies do not always promote justice or help individuals to be productive. Similarly, as hard as they try, schools, churches, and charitable groups do not always succeed in enhancing individual development. Some families can be dysfunctional, too, not fostering the kind of relationships and individual growth that healthy families do.

As social scientists study these and other institutions, they often point to flaws in them that they believe could be corrected through taking some appropriate action. When social scientists make recommendations that affect public life, their purpose for writing changes from informing their peers about their research to participating in civic discourse. They turn from the professional realm that normally absorbs most of their time and interest to the public realm, an openly political realm in which their recommendations might have real consequences in the lives of real people.

There are several genres in which social scientists might write about their opinions and recommendations. One would be an article for a popular magazine (as opposed to a professional journal). Another would be a newspaper article or editorial, often called an "opinion piece." Still another possible genre is called the "position paper," typically written for government officials and sometimes the public to influence them to adopt recommendations the writer might make.

Although position papers are often identified mainly with the writing that political scientists do, other social scientists—including economists, anthropologists, sociologists, social workers, psychologists—all might have occasion to make important contributions to the formation of public policies and programs. For example, suppose a state has the luxury of a budget surplus and its legislature is debating what to do with the extra funds. An economist might prepare a position paper recommending a reduction in the state property tax or sales tax, showing how the reduction would affect future state revenues and the general economy of the state. A social worker might write a position paper recommending increased funding for state agencies serving unemployed and homeless persons and people whose job skills need to be upgraded. A psychologist might argue for creating and staffing more public mental health clinics. An anthropologist could plead for a bigger budget to preserve sites in the state where remnants of prehistoric cultures have been discovered. The expertise of social scientists can sometimes magnify their voices in the political process and persuade legislators and the public to take actions they might not otherwise think of. By writing effective position papers, then, social scientists can use rhetoric in the way that it was first designed to be used—as a way of influencing the body politic.

As you prepare for your career, it is important for you to consider how you could apply your knowledge to the analysis of real problems that we face as members of the various overlapping communities we belong to. As you learn to create solutions to problems and recommend those solutions persuasively to the people who can implement them, you will see how your developing expertise in a field could have an impact in the lives of other people besides yourself and professional peers. In this chapter, you will learn some basic steps for writing position papers and opinion pieces to be read by the general public.

WRITING A POSITION PAPER

DEFINE AND LIMIT THE PROBLEM

The first step in writing a position paper is to define and limit the problem carefully. Most social problems are complex and therefore require multi-faceted solutions. Consider, for example, the problem of violent juvenile gangs in urban areas. The factors that might lead youth to join gangs are many, including lack of strong family ties, low self-esteem, unemployment and economic despair, peer pressure, racial discrimination, learning disabilities or low motivation to succeed in school, and lack of wholesome leisure time activities. Once youths have formed gangs, other factors could contribute to their destructiveness, including such things as too few police officers, easy access to firearms, inadequate detention and reform facilities, crowded court dockets, or laws with lenient penalties for adolescents. When you see how complex the problem of gangs is, you realize that it would probably take volumes to write a comprehensive position paper recommending solutions that would even start to scale back this problem, let alone get rid of it. Making a problem like this manageable obviously will require the efforts of a number of professions, all working together to attack it from different angles.

The complexity and intractability of most social problems means that writing an effective position paper will usually require you to limit your definition of the problem. So, for example, rather than defining the problem as "gangs," you could define it more narrowly by focusing on one of the factors that lead to the formation of gangs or contribute to their destructiveness. It will be most helpful, too, to focus on factors that could be affected by a public policy or program. For instance, you could focus on the shortage of police officers or the easy availability of firearms, since government officials have the power to appropriate money to hire more officers and to write laws regulating access to firearms.

However, if you see these measures as striking at the branch rather than the root of the problem, you might instead focus on factors that make some youth susceptible to the pressure to join gangs, such as low self-esteem, lack of success in school, or lack of constructive leisure time activities. You might choose these because you think it is possible to create educational and civic programs that could ameliorate the factors that predispose youth to join gangs. By selecting one part of this problem to study and take a position on, you would make your task manageable and you would be more likely to propose a clear and workable solution for decision makers to consider and act on.

RESEARCH THE PROBLEM

Once you have defined the problem, the next step is to learn more about it. Your two most likely sources of knowledge are documents and people who are experts on the subject you plan to write about.

Read documents. You may find most of what you need to know about the problem in documents, either at a library or at an institution that has something to do with the problem, such as a government agency, a workplace, or a charitable organization. The recency of publication, the carefulness of the research, the generalizability of any findings, and the political agenda of the writer could all be important for you to consider as you determine how much faith to place in any documents you use.

Documents from another institution could well become an important source of information as you work on defining the problem and developing solutions. For example, suppose your city council is debating whether or not to continue contributing a fraction of its budget to a privately run organization in your area that provides food and shelter to homeless persons. In the past, the city has chosen to make a contribution to this private organization rather than establish its own food and shelter operation, but now some citizens have objected that it is not the proper role of city government to contribute to private welfare services. To study this problem in order to write a position paper about it, you could check the records of the food and shelter organization (with permission of course) to determine how much of its total operating budget comes from the city; how many people it serves each year; how many people it could not serve if it didn't have the city's contribution; and who else contributes to the organization and how much. With facts like these, gleaned from the organization's own documents, you would be in a better position to analyze the nature of the problem and to think about possible solutions.

Consult experts. In addition to reading pertinent documents, it is important to learn from people who are close to the problem and therefore know a lot about it from their experience with it. If these experts are local, you may be able to interview them. For example, you could easily interview the directors of the food and shelter organization; you could also interview the mayor and members of the city council to learn about their reasoning in voting funds for the organization in the past. If the experts you would like to interview are more distant, you may still be able to reach them by phone, letter, or e-mail.

EVALUATE POSSIBLE SOLUTIONS

Once you have limited and defined the problem in a manageable way, you are ready to begin formulating solutions. But clearly it won't do to formulate easy "pie-in-the-sky" solutions that have no chance of being accepted. This means you will also have to evaluate the solutions you formulate so that you can offer those that have a good chance of being accepted. Obviously, solutions have a higher chance of being chosen and implemented if they are feasible (that is, they *can* be implemented and are likely to work); if the benefits are worth what it will cost to obtain them; and if the public can be persuaded to go along with implementing the solution. Let's examine these three interrelated criteria for evaluating solutions.

Feasibility. Solutions must actually be workable, given the power and resources that public officials or other administrators possess and are willing to use to solve a problem. If you identify part of the gang problem as poor parenting, you could decide that one solution would be to require all people who plan to have children to take courses in how to be parents, courses like how to teach their children to be able to resist negative peer pressure. Some reflection on this solution, however, would probably lead you to decide that this solution is simply not workable. How would you identify the people who should take the courses? How would you pay for creating and staffing the course? How would you ensure that people took it, or if they did, that they learned what they were supposed to? Even if you could achieve the initial steps, how could you guarantee the course would have the desired effect? This solution simply would not be practical.

If, however, you identify the most important part of the problem as a lack of constructive leisure time activities for children and teens to engage in, you may decide that a solution is locating or constructing more sports facilities, creating more after-school drama, music, and special interest groups for young people to be involved in, and getting people to work as coaches for sports or as leaders and teachers for other activities after school. This solution might be feasible, provided there are funds and people, either paid employees or volunteers, that can be employed in this cause, and provided that the right officials and the public could be persuaded to see the solution as feasible.

Cost-effectiveness. A very good way to demonstrate that a solution is feasible is to determine what it will cost to implement the solution and then to estimate the value of the benefits that should come from the solution. If the value of the benefits is greater than the cost, then the cost of implementing the solution may be attractive to decision-makers. Suppose you decided to propose that your city should provide two recreation facilities where young people could play sports or engage in other activities that would keep them off the streets. After some research, you could calculate the cost of building, renovating, or renting existing facilities, providing them with equipment, and staffing them with leaders, coaches, and teachers. Then you would attempt to determine the monetary benefits of this solution. It would be difficult, but with some research you might determine the city would eventually save money now being spent on police patrols, repairs of vandalized property, the creation of juvenile detention facilities, the juvenile justice system, and social service workers. If you could show that the costs would lead to measurable financial benefits, your solution would probably stand a better chance of being accepted. In this example, you might not be able to show that the city would save a lot of money, but you could argue that the money currently being spent on apprehension and punishment of gang members could be better spent on preventing gang activity in the first place.

Political Persuasiveness. Although it is important to argue for the feasibility and the cost-effectiveness of a solution in a position paper, these arguments may not count for much if you have misjudged the political climate and the attitudes of the people to whom you will be presenting your solution. Many people inside as well as outside government, for example, are simply not convinced that government can do much to prevent the gang problem. They do not view it as part of government's role to sponsor recreational facilities and hire people or seek volunteers to work with youth. They believe such activities are the proper role of churches, schools, private organizations, and the family. With beliefs like these, they are more likely to see solutions to gangs in stricter laws, more police officers to enforce the law, and more public spending for jails and prisons. You must always carefully analyze your audience and determine whether or not your proposal will be persuasive to them, given the political beliefs and assumptions they have.

RECOMMEND ONE OR MORE SOLUTIONS

As you analyze the problem, you will likely think of more than one solution that could be proposed. As you evaluate each solution, you should identify one that you think will be most feasible, most cost-effective, and most likely to win favor in the given political climate. However, you may believe that more than one of your solutions is workable, and you might consider offering ranked recommendations in the event that the audience for your position paper will be able to implement more than one solution. Remember, however, that you should argue forcefully for the solution you deem best. The whole aim of a position paper is to take a position, not to waffle after you have carefully researched the problem and evaluated the possible solutions.

DRAFT THE POSITION PAPER

After you have analyzed the problem carefully and chosen one or more workable solutions, the final step in producing a position paper is to write it. Two considerations are of prime importance in planning the paper: level of language and organization. As with other writing, your purpose and your audience will determine what you should do.

Level of language. Consider your audience carefully as you compose the sentences and paragraphs of your position paper. Remember that they may not share your expertise and the vocabulary that people in your field generally use. You may need to find synonyms for specialized terms or at least define and illustrate terms carefully before using them repeatedly in your paper. Use shorter sentences than you would generally use in writing for peers in your field. If you are writing for the general public, make your tone less formal as well; it may be appropriate to use some anecdotes, even personal ones, in addition to the statistics or other data you use to make your point. You want to move your audience to action, so in some cases it may be helpful to appeal to their emotions as well as their ability to reason, so long as the appeal is not manipulative. After completing a draft of your position paper, seek feedback from someone who knows the intended audience well or is already a part of that audience to see if the language you have chosen is understandable and makes the impact you desire.

Organization. A position paper can take many forms. If it is to be read by the public, a brief, simple, clear organization is probably best, since many will not likely have the patience to puzzle out a long, complex structure. If it is to be published in a magazine or newspaper, the paragraphs should be short because they will be displayed in narrow columns. The scholarly apparatus of footnotes or parenthetical references can usually be omitted for publication in popular periodicals, although you should be prepared to name your sources of information if asked. You may also work them into the text of the paper; for example, you might write, "A recent survey sponsored by a coalition of local businesses has shown. . . ."

For a more formal position paper that will be read by legislators or heads of organizations, the structure might be longer and more complicated, but it should use principles of document design to make the information accessible (see Chapter 11). For example, it would be wise to use headings that increase the accessibility of the desired information. Features such as numbered or bulleted lists or boldface and italic print can also help draw attention to key points. Important numerical data can often be presented in tables or graphs that let the reader quickly grasp relationships between different bits of data (see Chapter 12). The longer the paper is, the more helpful it is to provide a summary of your position and a table of contents to your document at the beginning to help busy readers get an overview of your position. In most cases, if you cite published sources, the position paper should have a list of references giving bibliographic citations for any printed materials you have consulted and names of people you have interviewed or contacted for information. Finally, if there is extra information that you did not put in the body of the paper but that would bolster the argument you make, it is appropriate to include it in one or more appendixes, so that readers who have the time to study your argument carefully can see all the data that led you to the solution you proposed.

8

ABSTRACTS, CRITIQUES, AND REVIEWS

CHAPTER OVERVIEW

After reading this chapter, you should be able to answer the following questions:

1. What is an abstract? Why is an abstract included in much social science writing? What are the characteristics of an abstract?
2. What is a peer review? What is usually included in one? How does a peer review help a writer improve a text?
3. What are book reviews? Why are they written? What are the usual parts of a book review?

The abstract, the critique, and the review are genres that you will have opportunity to write in both as a student and as a professional. These three kinds of writing have one thing in common: Each one requires you to size up and state succinctly what a document is about. In an abstract, that's all you do; no evaluative comments are included. In a critique or a review, however, you not only summarize the parts of an article, book, or other document, you also offer your opinion about their value. Knowing how to write in each of these genres is important because each one plays an important role in constructing the shared body of knowledge in any field. The critique does this by evaluating documents before they are published. Abstracts and reviews do this by offering members of the field an efficient way to keep up with the endless flow of new publications and to evaluate their usefulness, because of their importance in shaping knowledge and making it accessible.

WRITING AN ABSTRACT

Abstract is another name for a summary. Most social science journals require the author of an article to submit an abstract with the article. The abstract is not only printed with the article; it is also included in print sources and electronic databases that students and other scholars can search when looking for information on a particular topic. A well-written abstract is

- Brief, usually only a paragraph
- Dense with information encoded in key words
- Comprehensive in scope, summarizing each section of the document
- Impersonal in tone and style

These characteristics make it more likely that a computer will match the user's search terms with key words in the abstract and retrieve it. They also make it more likely that readers will be able to read the abstract and judge at a glance whether or not the entire article is pertinent to their research and worth reading in its entirety.

To write a good abstract, you have to have a good sense of your main point and of the structure of your document; you need to be able to state precisely what each part contributes to the whole. This means that the best time to write an abstract is after you have completed the entire document. If your document is a report of empirical research, it will likely have the following parts:

- An introduction that states a problem, question, or hypothesis to be investigated
- A description of methods, including participants, procedures, and materials
- A description of results
- A discussion of the significance of the results.

In sum, an abstract should do the following:

- Make sense by itself; it should be a miniature version of the paper, not omitting important points, not adding things that aren't in the paper, and not distorting the emphasis given to any part.
- Be specific; it should give details about the purpose, the scope, the methods used or the literature surveyed, the results, and the conclusions or implications.
- Be coherent and concise; it should move from point to point in a way that the reader can follow, with no wasted, empty words.
- Avoid evaluating; the author should present as objectively as possible what the entire paper is about and let the reader draw his or her own conclusions about the usefulness of the research.

- Be impersonal; it should not use the pronouns "I" or "we" or adopt a familiar, conversational tone.

WRITING A CRITIQUE

In Chapter 1, you learned that a researcher's new contribution to the literature of a field generally goes through a process of peer review before it is accepted for publication. The goal of this process is to ensure that writers will meet their disciplines' high standards for following research methods, analyzing and interpreting data, reasoning, and writing. Typically, a manuscript will be reviewed by at least two reviewers in the writer's field as well as by one or more editors at the journal or press that receives the manuscript. After review, the manuscript is usually returned to the writer with suggestions for revision. These suggestions might take the form of both marginal notations on the manuscript and written critiques in which the reviewers and editor describe in some detail the strengths and weaknesses of the manuscript and suggest ways to improve it. These critiques are meant for the writer only, not for a broader audience. After reading the critiques, the writer usually makes substantial revisions, sometimes negotiating details of content, organization, and style with the editor. Criticism of this kind is positive and helpful because it strengthens a document before it is finally published.

While you are still in college, probably very little, if anything, of what you write will be published in professional journals or by academic presses. (However, many campus departments and organizations sponsor undergraduate writing contests and sometimes journals, so you could very well aim to submit some of your best papers for judging or publication in local forums.) Even though most of your academic writing won't be published, it will be made public in the sense that it will be read by others. Your primary audience in most academic writing tasks is the instructor who assigned the writing. Your goal obviously is to submit quality work, and one way you can improve your written work is to solicit feedback from knowledgeable peers—your classmates, for example, or tutors in your campus writing center. Your teachers may even require that you show early drafts of your writing to others to receive feedback that will help you make your final draft stronger.

Just as you may solicit feedback from peers, you should be prepared to give helpful criticism, oral or written, to others about their writing. Because writing assignments vary widely, the kind of criticism you give to a classmate will depend on what the student has been asked to do; it will also depend on the criteria the instructor will use to evaluate each student's performance. The best place to begin any critique, therefore, is with careful scrutiny of the assignment's requirements and the evaluation criteria. If these are unclear, ask the instructor for more information. Most teachers want to get good writing from their students and therefore should be willing to clarify their instructions. Many instructors will also provide models of the kind of writing they are seeking with a given assignment. By studying the model, you can usually answer your own questions about appropriate format, organization, length, level of detail, and style.

As you evaluate an early draft of a classmate's paper, you will usually need to think about the following characteristics of the writing.

1. Focus. Depending on the type of assignment, the focus might be called the "thesis statement," the "purpose," the "claim," the "point," or some other name that indicates that a piece of writing is generally *about* something—it is generally limited to a particular aspect of a broad topic and the writer generally takes a particular position or point of view. No paper can say something about everything, and a paper that just wanders about, touching on this and that, but never asserting anything in particular, leaves you wondering what the reader is supposed to learn from it. To help you criticize the focus of a paper, ask questions such as these:

- Is the writer's focus clearly stated in a prominent position?
- Is the focus limited enough for the kind and length of paper?
- Is the focus evident throughout the paper, or does the paper seem to wander?
- How could the writer sharpen the focus?
- Could you state the thesis in your own words?
- Is the position the writer takes a significant and valid one?

2. Support. Once you have determined the focus of a paper, you should check how the writer supports his or her point of view. Support for a particular focus might take the form of general reasoning, of evidence drawn from authoritative sources, of data created by research methods, or of personal experience. To determine the relevance of the support, ask yourself such questions as these:

- Is the support appropriate for this kind of paper?
- Is the support relevant?
- Is it credible and reliable?
- Is it sufficient to make the writer's point?
- Has the writer taken into account contradictory evidence or simply ignored it?
- Does the support go into enough detail or is it too general?
- How could the writer make the support stronger?

3. Organization. The organization of a paper will depend on a lot of factors, including any directions the instructor gave in the assignment (or implied in the model, if one is given). The organization of a particular paper might be chronological if the paper is about the past or steps in a process. The organization might proceed from a problem to a solution, from a cause to an effect, or from an effect to a cause. It might compare two things point by point, or it might consider all the points related to one before proceeding to the other. It might divide something into its parts or classify a number of related things. Whatever it does, the organization of a paper should be congruent with the purpose and focus of the paper and help to advance the claim the writer is making. The reader should be able to discern the organization and should feel that the paper moves smoothly from part to part. To help you criticize the organization of someone's writing, consider these questions:

- Could you outline the paper?
- If the writer has outlined the paper, does the outline match the text?
- Has the writer chosen the best order to present points in?
- Are major points obscure, not given enough emphasis or space?
- Are less important points given too much emphasis?
- Would some points fit better somewhere else in the paper?
- Should some parts be deleted because they don't really fit in?
- Does the writer show connections between parts?
- Where could the writer strengthen the connections?
- Are headings appropriate? Would they improve the reader's ability to perceive the organization?
- How could the writer improve the organization?

4. Audience. All good academic writing is for somebody, and it is pitched at an appropriate level for the intended reader. All of the preceding elements— focus, support, and organization—must be considered when you evaluate the appropriateness of the writing for the audience. Ask yourself questions such as these:

- What readers does the paper address?
- What are the audience's expectations and needs?
- Has the writer taken the audience's knowledge, background, and experience into account?
- Will the audience find the particular focus appropriate and interesting?
- Will the audience find the support sufficient, relevant, and reliable?

- Will the organization help the audience understand the writing?
- What improvements in the paper would help the audience understand it better?

5. Format, style, and mechanics. The format of a paper includes such things as the overall appearance, the line spacing, the margins, the page numbering, and so forth. The format will vary with the genre assigned and the instructor's requirements. For example, some professors want a cover sheet on each paper with the title, course name, and your name in designated places. Others want your name, the course number, and the date in the upper right-hand (or left-hand) corner of the first page. Some want the pages numbered at the top, others at the bottom; still others don't care. Some professors are sticklers for one-inch margins; others are less fussy. Be sure you understand the instructor's preferences and instructions, if any, before proceeding to criticize the format of a classmate's paper.

If the instructor expresses no preferences and if the particular genre doesn't require any particular changes, check to see if the paper follows these general conventions:

- Is the text double-spaced?
- Does it have one-inch margins? (the default margins on most word processors)
- Does it have a ragged (unjustified) right margin?
- Has the writer paginated according to some consistent plan? (word processors offer several conventional choices)
- Is the body of the text in a 12-point serif font for the body of the paper?
- Are headings used correctly and appropriately?

Style refers mostly to the elements of writing at the sentence level, including choices about usage and punctuation. It can also refer to the institutional style a writer is expected to follow in a particular field. Writers have many choices to make in creating the style of a particular paper. Depending on the audience and purpose, some choices are better than others. *Mechanics* refers to those elements of writing that are purely arbitrary. It includes such things as using capitalization, brackets, ellipses, and italics correctly or following a particular style guide's rules for writing numbers, citing sources, and creating bibliographies. In evaluating style and mechanics, once again, you should do all you can to learn the instructor's requirements and preferences. (No checklist of questions will be given here.)

Usually the best way to note problems with format, style, and mechanics is to mark them directly on the draft of the paper you are criticizing, rather than devote a section of a formal written critique to these matters. It's important to note, however, that matters of format and style belong to the part of the writing process called editing, and they may not be as important in the early stages of writing as focus, support, organization, and appropriate adaptation for the audience. There is usually little point in editing writing that still needs a lot of work on focus and organization, for example.

To suggest a delay in criticizing the style, however, is not to imply that correctness in format, style, and mechanics is unimportant. In the final product correctness is very important, because a lot of small mistakes can interfere with the reader's ability to see the focus of a paper and to appreciate its support and organization. So, as a critic of others' writing, be sure that you do point out any serious problems or patterns of error that you notice in your peer's writing, especially if you are criticizing a near-final draft. But it usually isn't necessary to copy-edit someone's paper line by line. Unless you have been asked specifically to edit the paper, in most cases you can simply point out the problems that you see and let the writer assume the major responsibility for correcting them.

A Caution about Being Tactful

The above criteria are intended to describe writing in general—something that doesn't really exist. Writing is always for a *particular* situation: a paper is written by a particular person for an identified audience in response to a specific assignment about a particular topic. So you must always consider the particulars any time you are asked to offer a verbal or written critique of a classmate's work. One thing that will remain constant, however, is the need to offer criticism with grace and tact. Most people feel possessive about their writing, and even when they want to make it better, they sometimes feel attacked and defensive if their critics take a domineering or sarcastic approach. Imagine yourself on the receiving end of your critique. Would you be offended by it, or would you be able to accept it because it is offered in a kindly way? Be as honest as you must in offering criticism, but be as gentle as you can, too.

WRITING A REVIEW

The process of peer review that you learned about in Chapter 1 does not end with publication. Once an article or book appears in print or online, it is subject to the scrutiny of all readers who take an interest in the topic. Although an article or book has already successfully passed pre-publication review, it will continue to be reviewed in both indirect and direct ways. The most common indirect way that publications continue to receive peer review is through other writers' references to and citations of the publications. As one writer uses the work of another in creating a new document, the later writer may disagree with the earlier one; they might also praise the work of earlier ones, using it as a foundation for their own work, or extending an idea from the earlier books or articles. In these indirect ways, the writing of an author continues to undergo a type of review.

Another common way of responding to new publications is through directly commenting on them. Many professional journals have a section that is something like the letters to the editor of a newspaper. Readers can write a formal response to a recently published article and submit it to the journal. In their comments they might praise the article, ask for clarifications, or question the methods, analysis, or interpretations of an article. Sometimes journal editors invite the writer whose work is under scrutiny to reply to these critiques. By reading such comments and responses in the current professional journals of your field, you can gain a good sense of what the important issues are and of how scholars disagree with and challenge each other. You will see how writers defend their thinking or concede the validity of their peers' criticisms. This give-and-take illustrates well how knowledge is socially constructed through the process of offering, receiving, and responding to criticism.

Another direct method of evaluating someone's work is the formal review. For recently published books, editors of most journals invite reviews from knowledgeable peers, to be published in a section of the journal devoted just to book reviews. Each reviewer summarizes and evaluates an assigned book in a brief format, often less than 1,000 words. By reading these short reviews, others in the field can learn a little about new books appearing in the field and determine whether or not they should get a copy of a particular book and read it for themselves. Book reviews are a good source of information for students completing research projects as well. By reading a brief review, you can determine at least three things about a book: (1) what the book's topic and basic argument is; (2) whether a professional peer judges the book to be reliable; and (3) whether it will be worth your time to read the book at length for the information it might add to your research project.

As you near graduation and become more familiar with your major field's body of knowledge and its standards for evaluating new knowledge, you may be assigned to write formal reviews of published works. This is a valuable assignment, both because it requires you to read new books in your field and because it gives you practice in writing in a professional genre. You will learn to read for the main ideas, to separate the generalizations from the details, to think critically about what you are reading, and to apply your field's standards in evaluating the importance of new ideas and research. Writing a review takes practice, especially because the genre typically gives you only a small space in which to sum up and evaluate what you have read.

The best way to approach writing a review is to gain an overall conception of what this genre of writing usually includes. If you are writing a review for a class, your instructor will usually outline what your review should include and a maximum length. If you are writing a review for a journal, the editor will supply specifications. In either case, your review would typically have these parts:

- The facts of publication (author, title, publisher, etc.)
- A statement of the book's purpose and scope
- A summary of the book's contents
- An evaluation of some of the book's strengths and weaknesses
- Your general recommendation of the value of the book

It's important to note that, with the exception of the facts of publication, these parts would not necessarily be found in a review in the order given here. They might be intermixed in various ways. For convenience, however, they will be discussed as listed above.

THE FACTS OF PUBLICATION

The first elements in any book review are the title, author, place of publication, publisher, and year of publication for the book. In addition, the total number of pages and the cost of the book are usually included. If the book is available in both hard cover and paperback editions, the price for each may be given. Sometimes the ISBN (International Standard Book Number) is included as well. These details give readers of the review information they can use to order the book if they decide they want to purchase a copy. Or, if they don't plan to buy it, they have enough information to find it in a library.

STATEMENT OF THE BOOK'S PURPOSE AND SCOPE

The usual way of beginning a book review is to describe as objectively as possible what the author or authors of the book have attempted to do. Don't fault the author or authors for not writing the book you would have written. Try to understand the book in terms of what the author stated he or she was attempting to do. A good place to locate a statement of the author's purpose is in the preface or introduction to the book. State for your readers the book's purpose and its major claim or claims. It would also be appropriate to state any assumptions that underlie the claims.

Describing the particular genre the book belongs to can also help readers understand its purpose; for example, if a book is based on a survey or several interviews, saying so at the start of the review will help readers better evaluate the judgments you make later in the review. It is also helpful to describe briefly the major divisions or the general organization of the book. For example, if the book has three main divisions, you might give their titles and briefly tell what each part includes.

SUMMARY OF THE BOOK'S CONTENTS

In summarizing the book's contents you must be selective, mainly because the typical length limit of a book review forces you to be brief. One way to be selective is to summarize the book's main points at a very general level, giving just enough of the details or examples the authors use to illustrate how the points are supported. It may be appropriate to give a few brief quotations that state very clearly important ideas or focuses of the book. Your summary should substantiate your own overall opinion of the book.

EVALUATION OF STRENGTHS AND WEAKNESSES

The foregoing parts of a review all tell readers what a book is about, but readers will also want to know what the reviewer thinks of the book. They will want to see praise for specific strengths and criticism of identifiable weaknesses—and usually a book has both strengths and weaknesses, though it might have more of one than the other. As you read a book you've been assigned to review, you should be thinking critically about what the author has done in writing it as well as about what the book actually states. Here are some questions that may guide you in evaluating the strengths and weaknesses of a book:

- Is the book based on methodologically sound research?
- Does it deal adequately with the issues it raises?
- Is the book's scope as inclusive as it should be?
- Is it written clearly and persuasively?
- Has the author drawn on credible sources?
- Has the author overlooked information that would have contributed something worthwhile to the book?
- Is the book suitable for the audience it is intended for?

You might devote one or two paragraphs of your review to strengths and another paragraph to weaknesses. Or you might comment on the strong and weak points of the book as you summarize it. If your overall recommendation of the book is positive, it is important not to give undue prominence to its faults. The amount of space you devote to discussing strengths and weaknesses ought to be proportionate to your general assessment of the book's value.

GENERAL RECOMMENDATION

The reviewer's general recommendation usually appears twice in the review: at the beginning and again at the end. Readers want to find out in the first few sentences of the review if your overall evaluation is positive, negative, or mixed. Be forthright in stating an opinion that you will then support through your summary and evaluation of specific strengths and weaknesses. At the end of the review, you can state your overall opinion again, this time knowing you have supported it with the facts you've included in the body of your review. If your overall opinion is a mix of positive and negative feelings, you should write a carefully qualified statement, balancing praise with criticism.

For example, you should let your readers know if the book is technical and difficult to read but would still have value for a certain group of readers who should take the time to struggle through it. If the book largely repeats what is already known but contributes a few important new ideas, then say what those ideas are. Your readers may ultimately disagree with your evaluation, but that is not a problem. By being a responsible critic, you perform a valuable service in perpetuating the conversation about a field's knowledge. Your review is like a turn in the conversation, which itself should invite still other responses.

9

RESUMES

CHAPTER OVERVIEW

After reading this chapter, you should be able to answer the following questions:

1. What is a resume? What is a *curriculum vitae*? How do they differ?
2. What is a one-column resume? What is a two-column resume?
3. What are the typical parts of any resume?
4. What should you keep in mind when formatting a resume?
5. What are some precautions you need to take when posting your resume online?
6. How does a scannable resume differ from a printed one?

TYPES OF RESUMES

A *resume* (from the French word *résumé*) is a summary of pertinent facts about you that you will often be asked to submit with a letter of application or to bring to an interview. In the academic world, a similar kind of summary goes by the Latin name *curriculum vitae* (often simply called *vita*), which means "course of life." Graduate and professional schools may ask you to submit a vita rather than a resume. The vita typically focuses on academic achievements, such as publications and scholarly activities and awards. Since it is a life-long record, it tends to be longer than a resume, especially as a person ages and has more achievements to list. The resume, on the other hand, is kept brief (usually only a page, occasionally two). Businesses and professional schools often ask for a resume. It tends to focus more on work experience and skills, though education and academic honors are included as well. Since the two kinds of documents are rather similar, and since at this point in your life you are more likely to have had the kinds of experiences that are usually recounted in a resume, the name *resume* will be used in the rest of this chapter.

Although employers normally request a traditional paper resume, electronic resumes are becoming common as well. Electronic resumes can speed up the process of being considered for a job. Once you post your resume on the Web, potential employers can search the Web using key words to locate you and other possible employees. Then, when they are looking for an employee with certain skills, they can search the database for all resumes that name the desired skills and retrieve the names and addresses of potential employees. Although this chapter will further describe online resumes, it will focus mainly on traditional printed resumes. Once you create a printed resume, you can reformat it to fit the online guidelines.

TRADITIONAL RESUMES

In the traditional resume, the design and visual attractiveness of the document matter much more than in most writing you do for college courses. You should refer to the elements of document design discussed in Chapter 11 as you view the examples of traditional resumes in this chapter. This chapter will also help you as you begin to apply the principles of design to your resume. As important as design is, however, you must first plan carefully what to include and how to organize the contents of your resume for the greatest impact.

ORGANIZATION OF THE TRADITIONAL RESUME

The organization you use for each resume depends on the particular job you are applying for. You should research the requirements for each job carefully so that you can tailor your resume to show how your qualifications match its specifications. In any case, your resume should quickly acquaint the reader with your abilities and strengths. An employer going through a stack of resumes typically spends only 15–20 seconds scanning each one, so he or she needs to be able to access your qualifications right away. Careful organization can help an employer notice your most important qualities.

Information in resumes is typically displayed in categories identified by headings. Within these categories, the facts can be displayed in list fashion with bullets drawing attention to particular items. You can also use concise paragraphs to summarize your work and experiences. Some categories of information are fairly standard on resumes, while others may vary according to your background and the immediate goals and audience for the resume. These standard and optional categories, including what each would contain, are described in the next section. The categories often come in the order given here, but this order is not fixed—you should vary your headings according to specific job requirements.

Contents of the Traditional Resume

Name and Contact Information (Standard). Every resume should display at the top your name, address, E-mail address, and telephone number(s). When listing more than one number, it is helpful to distinguish them as daytime or evening numbers and to note at which a message can be left. Employers might also appreciate a fax number if you have one. Some college students list permanent contact information in this section as well because their local information frequently changes.

Career Objective (Optional). Some people list a career objective immediately after their name and contact information. However, most career experts advise you to omit the objective because it can limit what an employer will consider you qualified to do. Consider whether you want to use precious space for an objective statement. If you choose to include one, you should customize your resume for each job you apply for by stating your career objective so that it matches what the employer has advertised for.

Trying to write a "one-size-fits-all" career objective can be hazardous. For example, stating your career objective too specifically (e.g., "to work as a tax attorney in a major corporate law firm") could backfire if an employer interpreted it to mean that you would not consider a different, but related, position. Stating it too broadly (e.g., "to manage personnel") might make it seem you are too vague about your career goals. Stating it too ambitiously (e.g., "to become Vice-President of International Marketing") may suggest you intend to use the available position as only a quick stop on your move up the corporate ladder. Consider your purpose and audience carefully when deciding whether or not to include this category in your resume at all. It often can be omitted without sacrificing much.

Educational History (Standard). At this stage of your life, your education will likely be the most prominent category of information after the heading. List the schools where you have studied in *reverse chronological order*, beginning with the university that you are now attending. For your current university, include your major (and minor, if you have one), your dates of enrollment, and your expected graduation date. If your GPA is admirable (generally anything over a 3.5), you may want to list it as well. Some students who don't have an impressive cumulative GPA may have a respectable one for the courses they have taken in their major. If that is the case with you, consider listing your major GPA only.

Some students also include relevant coursework, class projects, or research under the education category. You could also list scholarships and academic honors here, or you could list them later in the resume with other awards and achievements. When listing the schools you have attended, do not go further into the past than high school. In fact, if you graduated from high school more than five years ago, consider omitting that part of your education. (As a general rule of thumb for updating your resume over the years, eliminate the older and less significant facts about yourself as you add more recent and more important achievements.)

Work Experience (Standard). You can organize your work experience by time (a *chronological* resume) or by skill sets (a *functional* resume). You may even choose to use a combination of these. Most career counselors recommend writing a chronological resume because it is easier for an employer to see your work history. If you have had steady work experience and several jobs like the one for which you are applying, write a chronological resume. For this type of resume, list your experiences starting with your current or most recent one and moving back in time. A chronological resume concentrates on day-to-day job responsibilities and can show your progress in a certain career field.

The work experience section of your resume can include full-time jobs, part-time jobs, internships, research or teaching assistantships, and perhaps even volunteer experience. (If you have a great deal of volunteer experience, consider creating a separate category for it in the resume.) Include only the most applicable experiences rather than listing every position you've held since high school. Or group your part-time or summer jobs in a cluster, without giving details about each.

List the following in the order given for each significant job:

- Your job title
- The name of the organization you worked for
- The location of the organization
- The dates of your employment

You could also list your supervisor's name with each job as a way of indicating whom the prospective employer could contact for a reference.

Especially when you have held few or no full-time jobs, it is important to put the best face you can on the jobs you have held but to do so without overstating what you really did. Employers may not be as interested in the number of years you have worked or the prestige of your jobs as they are in the skills and personal attributes your work experience has given you. Emphasize how your employment has instilled in you such things as the ability to relate well with others, to communicate, to accept responsibility and follow through, to organize, to solve problems, to meet deadlines, to work with various kinds of equipment, and so forth. Describing specific tasks you did on each job will show what skills you have acquired.

When you present your information in your resume, you should use telegraph writing style; that is, you will seldom use complete sentences. Rather, you will write words and phrases that present the information about yourself as clearly and concisely as possible. Keep punctuation to a minimum, using mostly commas. Also, make sure that the items you list are conceptually and grammatically parallel. For example, "Developed preschool evaluations," a verb phrase, is not parallel with "Recreational leader," a noun phrase. Capitalization in the resume will vary from capitalization in the accompanying letter. In the resume, you may use capital letters for degrees you've earned or expect to earn, names of courses, job titles, or other significant words. In the cover letter, however, capitalization should conform to standard rules for common and proper nouns.

Skills (Optional). You may have other skills that an employer would value but which you didn't acquire working at specific jobs. For example, through study or travel you may be fluent in speaking, reading, and writing one or more foreign languages. In school or on your own you may have acquired skills in working with various kinds of computer software. Through school or volunteer projects, you may have developed expertise in various research methods and in statistics or in writing and editing. This kind of information deserves prominence in your resume, and a skills section is one option for presenting it.

Accomplishments and Awards (Optional). When you are writing a resume, it is no time to be modest about your achievements. As Babe Ruth once said, "If you done it, it ain't braggin'." Obviously, you shouldn't seem vain by making more out of accomplishments than is warranted, but do state the facts. In this section, you can list scholarships and academic awards if you haven't already listed them with your educational history. This may also be the place to describe volunteer work if you haven't included it elsewhere. You may also list civic awards, special recognition from employers, memberships and leadership positions you have held in societies and clubs, or any extracurricular activities that distinguish you. Don't go further back than high school and do weigh the merits of listing some of your honors by considering how impressive they are likely to be to a prospective employer. (That you were the Homecoming Queen or the Most Preferred Man in your senior year of high school is probably not relevant for most jobs.) The heading you give this section can vary depending on what it emphasizes.

DESIGN OF THE RESUME

Layout. Think of the resume as being arranged in "chunks" of information with indented "layers" in the chunks to help readers quickly find what they are seeking. The layout should have a more vertical than horizontal feel to it. Horizontal texts, like this page, are intended for you to read from left to right, line by line, straight through from top to bottom. A resume, however, is a document that should permit random access of information; that is, a reader should be able to scan up or down it quickly, reading the headings to locate needed information. Within the major sections, the lines of text should be short and arranged in layered columns, so that left-to-right reading takes very little time. Generally, resumes have two main columns, with the column at the left containing the headings and the column on the right containing the details. In order to keep a resume to one page, however, it may become necessary to use the width of the page for the details, with headings above each category of details in a one-column format.

White space. Whether you use a one- or a two-column format, be sure to use white space to keep the resume from looking too dense or cluttered. Use indentations within columns to show how the most specific information is subordinate to more general information. Avoid creating "windows" of white space (empty spaces surrounded by print on all sides). Most of the white space should be on the sides and top and bottom, but leave some between the sections of the resume as well.

Graphical devices. Use graphical devices sparingly. Typically the only ones you should use on a resume are horizontal or vertical rules and bullets. Consider your audience and purpose carefully before deciding to include other graphics such as icons or text boxes. A neat, simple appearance is preferable to one that aims to show off all your printer's fonts.

Fonts and Point Sizes. Here are some guidelines to remember when choosing fonts and type sizes:

- *Choose a typeset font.* With contemporary word processors, you can achieve a more professional look in your resume by choosing a font that is used in typesetting (e.g., Times New Roman or Garamond) rather than a font that looks like it was produced by a typewriter (e.g., Courier or Letter Gothic).

- *Choose a serif font for the body (you may choose a sans-serif font for headings).* Always choose a serif font for the body of the resume, though you may use a sans serif font for your name and contact information and for the headings, if you wish. Don't use a script or novelty font.

- *Use no more than two fonts.* In general, you should not use more than two fonts on your resume, though you may put some words in boldface or italics. For example, your name and the headings can be put in boldface to give them more weight and thus visual prominence.

- *Use bigger type for name and headings.* Your name and the headings will also appear more prominent if you put them in a bigger point size.

- *Use type sizes between 9 and 12 points.* In general, other than your name and headings, the resume should be in a point size between 9 and 12. If you are faced with using a point size of 8 or smaller to fit all the information on one page, it is time to leave something out. You may also consider making the resume two pages, but you should realize that a busy reader might not have time to look at both pages.

PAPER AND PRINTING

When applying for a job, internship, graduate school, or other opportunity important to your future, be prepared to spend a few extra dollars to make the best impression possible. You should have your resume laser-printed on high quality bond paper that is white or off-white. If your resume is accompanied by a cover letter, or sent in a business-sized envelope, these should be from the same paper stock.

When you think your resume is nearly done, print and proofread a draft of it; then ask a few people to read it for correctness before printing the final draft. If you make any changes from their feedback, proofread your resume again. Remember that a single spelling, grammatical, or typographical error may be enough reason for a would-be employer to eliminate you from consideration. If you make any changes from their feedback, proofread your resume again.

10

LETTERS AND MEMOS

CHAPTER OVERVIEW

After reading this chapter, you should be able to answer the following questions:

1. How does a letter of application differ from a letter of intent?
2. What are the typical parts of a letter of application?
3. What is full-block style? What is semi-block style?
4. What is involved in writing a letter of intent?
5. Where are memos used? What are they typically like? When would a person choose to write a paper memo rather than send an E-mail?

As you approach the end of your undergraduate years, important decisions await you. Will you seek a job? If so, where? Will you go to graduate school? If so, what is involved in applying? The answers to these questions are likely to involve writing in some form. For example, if you are ready to apply for a job, you will generally send out letters of application. If you plan to apply for graduate or professional school, you will very likely have to compose a letter of intent or personal statement to send with other required materials. This chapter outlines principles of form and content, as well as steps to composing, that will help you create effective letters of application or intent.

The letter of application or intent helps you start on the path toward your professional goals. Once you are established in your profession, you will learn to write in many other genres, one of which is the memorandum. Since the memo is common in virtually all professions, this chapter also gives some brief instruction about the form and content of memos, both print and electronic. Your instructor may have you write some memos as a way of practicing this genre and communicating with teacher or classmates about assignments in your class.

LETTERS OF APPLICATION

A letter of application is usually accompanied by a resume (see Chapter 9). In fact, the letter of application is sometimes called a "cover letter" because it allows you to draw the reader's attention to the resume and to elaborate on some of the facts listed in it. Generally your purpose in sending a letter and resume is to get an interview with the recipient or the chance to take the next step in the application process. Letters of application may be sent not only for a job, but also for internships, scholarships, grants, or other opportunities you want to apply for. Whatever their purpose, they generally take the same form as a standard business letter. That is, they have each of the parts listed below, and they incorporate the design elements described below. Knowing about the letter's parts and design is not sufficient for creating a successful letter, however, so this chapter also includes advice for composing your letter.

PARTS OF THE LETTER

Heading. Except when you are writing on letterhead stationery (which is already printed with your return address), the first element of a business letter is the heading, which consists of your address and the date. Give your complete street address on the first line; the city, state, and zip code on the next line; and the date on the third line. The name of the state can be abbreviated using the standard two-letter abbreviation used by the U.S. Postal Service. The date should be written out completely, using the full name of the month rather than an abbreviation or a numeral (e.g., September 15, 2015, or 15 September 2015, but not Sept. 15, '15 or 9/15/15). Here are two sample headings:

> 726 Pleasantview Drive   1703 Auburn Street #202
> Cove Village, CA 96346   Richardson, TX 75081
> August 31, 2015   31 August 2015

Inside Address. After spacing at least twice (or more, depending on the length of your letter), write the name, title, and complete address of the person who is to receive your letter. If you don't know the name, it is acceptable to use just the title of the person you wish to receive your letter (e.g., Vice-President for Human Resources, or Chair of the Scholarship Committee). Here are two sample inside addresses:

> Anthropology Department Chair   Ms. Lisa Tanner-Hawkins
> University of Utah   Director of Human Resources
> 270 South 1400 East Room 102   National Information Systems
> Salt Lake City, UT 84112   259 Research Drive
>   Longbrook, NY 20153

Salutation or Greeting. Space twice after the inside address and write "Dear _____:" (Note that the salutation is punctuated with a colon, not a comma, unless you know the person to whom you are writing.) Fill in the blank with the title and last name of the person you are addressing. If the person goes by a title such as *Dr., Professor,* or *President,* you should use that. If no special title is used, use the standard polite forms of address. For a man, obviously, you will use the title *Mr.;* for a woman, you should use *Ms.,* unless you know the woman prefers to be addressed by *Miss* or *Mrs.* If you know the person well enough, you may use a first name.

Sometimes a person will use only initials or will have a first name that may be given to either sex. If you haven't met the person or can't otherwise determine the person's gender, the best option is to use the complete name in the salutation. For example, if you didn't know whether Taylor Johnston was a man or woman, you could write "Dear Taylor Johnston:"

Companies or graduate programs will recognize applicants who do some research to find the name of a department chair, director, or manager. Using a name is always preferred to using a title or position. If you cannot find the name of the person who will read your letter, however, you may use a title in the salutation, as in "Dear Graduate Coordinator." Or, in place of the greeting, you may write an attention or subject line, such as one of the following:

Attention: Recreational Programs Director
Subject: Advertisement for Summer Interns
Re: Editorial Position

So-called generic greetings of an earlier era, such as "Gentlemen," "Dear Sir," or "Dear Sir or Madam" are no longer used because they don't adequately reflect the realities or the language used in today's business world.

The Body. Beginning two lines under the greeting, write the body of the letter. In a letter of application, the body is generally three or four paragraphs long, each with a definite role to play in raising your reader's interest and persuading him or her to consider your application more carefully.

First paragraph. In the first paragraph, you should name the position or opportunity you are seeking and, particularly for a job, how you learned about it. Include the name of a professor, former employer, or other contact if he or she has encouraged you to pursue the job. Mentioning a contact can impress a potential employer. Employers also want to know how the news of an opening becomes known. If you saw an advertisement, mention it; if you heard about it from another person, mention that. If you do not know there is an opening and are writing on the chance that there might be, briefly explain why you want to work for the organization. End this paragraph by stating in a few words why you feel you are qualified for the position or opportunity.

Middle paragraphs. In the middle paragraph or paragraphs, elaborate on your qualifications. You might devote one paragraph to your educational preparation and another to your work or volunteer experience. Be specific. In addition to writing, "I am a well-organized, efficient worker," provide details that *show* the reader that you are. For example, you might write, "During my internship at Clyde Museum, my public relations team increased museum attendance by 30% through our history awareness campaign." You may also want to address possible reservations that your prospective employer may have about hiring you. Put yourself in the reader's position and consider what he or she might be concerned about or interested in.

Of course, be sure to carefully select what you include; you don't want to oversell yourself, and you want to keep the letter to a page. Remember that your letter works in tandem with your resume to give the reader as full a picture as possible of your experience and abilities. By presenting and elaborating on some well-chosen details about yourself in the letter, you hope to interest the employer enough to gain an interview, at which you can elaborate further.

Final paragraphs. In the final paragraph, refer the reader to your resume and politely request further action. Indicate when you will be available for an interview and express hope that you will hear from the employer soon. If the organization is in another city to which you will soon be traveling, ask to have an appointment during your stay. Sound a confident but not too aggressive tone in the closing lines of your letter.

Complimentary Close. Two lines under the body of the letter, you will write one of several common closings that will precede your signature. For a formal letter addressed to someone you are not well acquainted with, the standard complimentary closes are listed below. Note that each is followed by a comma:

- Sincerely,
- Sincerely yours,
- Yours truly,
- Very truly yours,
- Respectfully,

If you are acquainted with the addressee, you could consider using "Cordially," or "Best regards."

Signature and Typed Name. After the complimentary close, space down four lines and type your complete name. Write your signature in the blank space above your typed name.

Enclosure Line. If you have enclosed something with the letter (and with an application letter you will generally enclose your resume) it is common to type the word "Enclosure" two lines after your name, flush with the left margin.

DESIGN OF THE LETTER

Layout. There are two ways to format a business letter: full-block style or semi-block style. In full-block style, all parts of the letter are aligned flush with the left margin. In semi-block style, the heading, complimentary close, and signature are aligned with each other and are placed right of the center of the page. In addition, in the semi-block style, the opening line of each paragraph can be indented five spaces.

The letter should have enough white space in it that it does not look formidable to read. Although paragraphs are single-spaced, you should double-space between paragraphs. To avoid giving the letter a top-heavy appearance, center the printed matter on the page. One way to introduce more white space at the top of the letter is to space several lines between the heading and the inside address. Between all other parts of the letter, however, you should leave only two lines of space. Margins on both sides and at the top and bottom of the letter should be at least one inch. Do *not* justify the right margin because doing so makes the letter more difficult to read.

Unlike a resume, a letter is not designed for random access. It is meant to be read line by line, from left to right, beginning at the top and moving to the bottom. Additional devices to draw attention to layout, such as boldface or headings, are generally not needed. In some cases, additional indentation and bullets might be used in a letter, but not often.

Fonts and Point Sizes. As with the resume, choose a serif font that looks professionally typeset (such as Times New Roman) rather than typewritten (such as Courier). The usual point size for a letter is 12, though you could use 11 or even 10 if doing so would help you keep the letter to one page. But be considerate of your reader and don't strain his or her eyesight! If you would have to use an even smaller point size to make your letter fit on a page, consider cutting parts of your letter. Only in rare cases should you send a two-page letter.

Paper and Printing. Laser print your letter on high quality bond paper of the same stock you use for your resume. The professional appearance of your letter makes an important first impression on your reader, so this is no time to be cheap or careless.

COMPOSING YOUR LETTER

Business letters have become a highly standardized genre. In a sense, this is good because the conventions to follow are quite clear-cut. However, it also could be detrimental because you may be tempted to lapse into formulaic, clichéd writing. Your application letter is generally your first contact with an employer or someone who has the ability to grant you the internship or scholarship you are seeking, so you want to make a good impression and distinguish yourself from other applicants. You want your own voice and personality to come through in your letter while still observing the conventions the genre entails. Use the letters in this section mainly for formatting guides; your letter's content should be presented in your own voice, not in words duplicated from a good example.

Prewriting. As in other writing tasks, an effective prewriting strategy is the first step to a successful final draft. Use a technique such as brainstorming, listing, or freewriting to generate as many facts about yourself as you can—anything you think might even remotely interest an employer or award committee. Write much more than you can possibly use because the very act of generating material may help you think more carefully about your strengths. With a lot of material to choose from, select the facts that best represent your qualifications. Plan how you can arrange and interpret these details about yourself to show why you would be the best choice for the job, the internship, the scholarship, or other opportunity.

Drafting. Write a longer first draft than you can use, then cut it down to size. Consider the order you present your ideas in: Is it logical and clear? Also consider how your sentences connect with each other; make transitions explicit.

Because the letter is about yourself, you will find that you need to say "I" in it frequently. There is nothing wrong or immodest about this. However, it can become monotonous if you begin every sentence with "I." Find ways to vary your syntax so that you do not need to start every sentence with a reference to yourself.

Revising and proofreading. Revise and edit carefully to make the letter correct and concise. Show a near-final draft to trusted professors, advisers, or tutors in your campus writing center. Incorporate worthwhile suggestions from them and then proofread with the utmost care. As with a resume, a single spelling, grammatical, or typographical mistake in a letter can be your undoing when the reader is looking for a reason to eliminate some contenders from consideration.

LETTERS OF INTENT AND PERSONAL STATEMENTS

A letter of intent or personal statement is usually part of an application for graduate or professional school, but sometimes it is also required for a scholarship or internship application. Despite its name, a letter of intent is usually not formatted as a letter: it has no inside address, salutation, or complimentary close, though it may have a heading and a signature. It is like an essay in both form and content, yet it is like a letter of application in important ways: it is about your qualifications, and its purpose is to persuade readers (usually a committee of professors) to choose you from among many other applicants for a position in the program you want to enter, or for an internship or scholarship.

In this chapter, it's not possible to delve into how letters of intent for law school might differ from those for an MBA program; instead, this chapter provides some general advice on how to make your letter best represent you. You should be able to get more particular advice from five sources:

1. The admissions offices at the schools you plan to apply to will tell you what form your statement must take, how long it can be, and the kinds of information the admissions committee is seeking.

2. BYU's Counseling and Career Center offers workshops specifically about researching and applying for graduate school. Mentors there can help you write genre-specific letters of intent.

3. A number of books available in libraries and bookstores give helpful advice for writing letters for particular kinds of graduate programs.

4. A professor or mentor in the field you want to enter can give you helpful feedback before you print and mail a final draft of your statement.

5. The instructions that accompany the application form for a scholarship or internship may tell you what to include in your letter.

IMPORTANCE OF THE LETTER

The letter of intent is one of the main parts of a typical application for graduate school. The other parts are usually an application form; a transcript of your undergraduate courses and grades; test scores from standardized aptitude and achievement tests such as the GRE, the LSAT, the GMAT, or the MCAT; letters of recommendation (usually three) from professors or others who can attest to your intellectual, social, and personal qualifications for graduate school; and a resume, or at least a list of work experience and extracurricular activities. Because you will be hurrying to submit all of these parts of the application by a certain deadline, you may be tempted to think you can toss off your personal statement in a few hours a couple of days before you have to mail it. Thinking that would be a big mistake.

The letter of intent is often the most important part of the application—in fact, it is the only one you still have some control over as application deadlines loom. By then your GPA is already pretty well determined, your test scores have already been calculated, and your letters of recommendation are beyond your control. But in your personal statement you can still say things about yourself that will not otherwise be apparent to the admissions committee. A strong personal statement, for example, can sometimes salvage an application that isn't distinguished by a high GPA or impressive exam scores. A poor statement, on the other hand, may sabotage an otherwise competitive application. Even when the other indicators of a successful application are strong, a highly effective personal statement may bring a bonus beyond mere admission—a scholarship or tuition waiver, for example. You should therefore plan to start several weeks early, if possible, to draft your letter of intent.

A well-written personal statement can also make or break your application for an internship or scholarship. In most cases, you will be competing with other applicants whose qualifications are about as strong as yours, so the statement is often the best chance you have to distinguish yourself from the others and impress the committee to choose you.

GENERATING SUBSTANCE THROUGH PREWRITING

Before you begin drafting your statement, generate a lot of possible material that you could use in it. Here are some questions to which you could freewrite answers:

1. What is your motivation for wanting an advanced degree or other award? What events in your life gave you that motivation? What feelings or impulses move you in this direction?

2. What are your strengths? How are they related to succeeding in the career you've chosen? What have you chosen to do in your courses and extracurricular activities to prepare yourself for the kind of career you want?

3. What significant experiences have you had that show you have the talents to succeed in a rigorous graduate program? What unique experiences and abilities would you bring to the school you are applying to? Why would you make the best use of a scholarship? Why do deserve the internship?

DRAFTING AROUND A THEME

Since the personal statement is a brief essay, it should have a clearly defined focus or theme. After generating ideas through prewriting answers to the above questions, you should be able to select a focus from all you've written and begin to draft your essay around that theme. For example, you could narrate a defining event or series of events in your life that helped crystallize a particular career choice for you. Then you can add brief descriptions of how other choices and experiences have prepared you for that career.

Another way to make an argument for your acceptance is to explain strengths you have that are not measurable by test scores and GPA. Things such as work and volunteer experience, interpersonal skills, bilingual and bicultural abilities, and the ability to be independent and self-motivated count with admissions and scholarship or internship committees, if you can show how these traits are relevant to the course of study you wish to pursue. Resist the temptation to spell out everything about your life, however. There is no need to repeat information that is available in other parts of your application, and there is generally a word limit for the statement anyway. Still another approach is to explain why your particular background and talents are a good match for unique courses the program offers. This means, of course, that you will have to research the various programs you plan to apply to and learn what special emphases they offer.

REVISING AND EDITING

Plan to spend a number of hours working on your statement over a period of two or three weeks. Draft a version, get feedback on it, and let it rest a few days. Then write another version, trying ideas others have given you. Continue seeking feedback and revising until you have a draft that includes particulars that you think best describe you. Work on the organization to make it clear and cohesive; the conceptual links between paragraphs should be apparent but not obtrusive.

As you edit to make your statement the right length, be alert to empty words you could cut and to stilted words or jargon that you would not likely use if you were speaking to the admissions committee. They are not looking to be impressed by a big vocabulary; instead, they want clarity. The importance of correct spelling, usage, and sentence structure can't be overstated. The ability to write well is extremely important in all kinds of graduate work, and the committee will judge your ability to succeed as a writer in graduate school by the quality of the writing in your personal statement. Mistakes can lower your ranking in the list of applicants. You and at least one other person should proofread your statement carefully before you mail it. As with other letters, laser print the final draft on high quality bond paper either white or off-white in color.

MEMOS

The memorandum (the plural is memoranda), or the memo for short, is a brief written form of communication used within an organization. Brevity, clarity, and efficiency in reading are its hallmarks. Memos differ from letters in that they have no salutation, no complimentary close, and generally no signature (although the writer sometimes writes his or her initials next to the "from" line). Instead, the memo has a heading indicating who the reader is, who the sender is, the date, and what the memo is about. This is a sample heading:

To:	All Faculty
From:	Travel Office
Date:	6 August 2015
Subject:	New Regulations for Travel Per Diem Allowance

In many organizations, special memo paper is printed with the "To," "From," and "Date" components already supplied, each followed by a blank line which the writer can fill in. These institutions also frequently have special memo envelopes designed for routing memos from one office or department to another. Organizations that you have worked for in the past may have had their own practices for creating and sending memos.

As e-mail is fast becoming the preferred medium for communicating within an organization, special memo stationery and envelopes are on the decline. Nevertheless, hard copies of memos (ones printed on paper) are still important in most organizations, particularly when a durable, portable record of the contents is needed. Memos originally composed in e-mail can be printed. Memos composed for paper circulation can also sent by e-mail, either as an attachment or directly within a message. Whether the original medium is paper or electronic, the general purposes for memos and many of the principles for composing them remain the same. This chapter focuses first on printed memos, then offers tips for using e-mail in a professional setting.

COMPOSING A MEMO

As in other rhetorical situations, begin writing a memo by asking yourself who your audience is and what your purpose is. With a memo, you may have multiple readers. Usually, a memo is addressed to just one person, however, and other intended readers are named in a line that may be headed "Copy" or "cc." (The "cc" stands for "carbon copy" and dates back to the days when typewriters were the principal office technology for writing, and carbon paper was what office workers used in place of a photocopy machine.) The "copy" line may come in the memo's heading or it may come after the body of the memo.

The purposes for memos are numerous and various. Here are some typical ones:

- To propose a course of action
- To report on an action

- To report on facts discovered through research
- To give a progress report
- To record and remind others of decisions made in a meeting or conversation
- To inform of a new policy or procedure
- To make announcements of general interest
- To ask questions
- To answer questions
- To summarize something—e.g., a document or meeting—for a busy person

Whatever the purpose, the goal is to say simply and briefly what you have to say. When little is at stake—when you are simply tossing out ideas for a few co-workers, for example—memos can be hastily written. Memos in government agencies, on the other hand, might become part of a paper trail that has legal or historical implications. The more important your audience or purpose, and the more important the contents are, the more carefully you should plan the wording and the design of your memo. For memos with potentially broad significance, it may take many hours of writing to achieve the right wording and the ease of reading that characterize a good memo.

DESIGNING THE MEMO

Memos usually have two parts: the heading and the body. A long memo communicating complex information might have a separate conclusion as well, summarizing the contents, drawing conclusions, or making recommendations. How much you need to design the visual structure of a memo depends largely on the length and complexity of the information it conveys. In very brief memos of only a paragraph or two, the need for design is minimal since most readers will be able to understand the entire contents in a few minutes. For a brief memo, the most helpful thing you can do is to write a clear and complete "Subject" or "Re" line in the heading. (*Re* is from Latin and means "concerning" or "about.") The subject line should sum up the memo's contents in a few memorable words.

For long memos, particularly those conveying complex information, a brief opening paragraph that gives an overview of the contents can help the reader significantly. This overview can correspond to internal headings in the memo that help busy readers locate desired information quickly. Another way to help the reader read efficiently is to use principles of document design (see Chapter 11). For example, internal headings can be placed in a separate column to the left of the text. Or they can be in boldface and underlined, then placed above sections of the text, either centered or on the left margin. Within sections of a memo, bulleted or numbered lists can present complex information in a more visual and useful fashion. White space between sections, around lists, and elsewhere also makes a long memo more readable because it relieves the formidable impression of a densely worded page.

E-MAIL ETIQUETTE

Increasingly, e-mail is used rather than paper memos in academic and professional settings to communicate between teacher and student, supervisor and employee, colleague and colleague. While just about everyone knows how to use e-mail for informal communication with friends and family, it's not the case that everyone knows how to use it in a more formal and professional setting. Here are some tips that will help you avoid having your e-mails deleted or misinterpreted as unprofessional, rude, or trivial.

- Be sure that your e-mail address includes your name or a short version of your name that is clear and unambiguous. A cute or suggestive e-mail address is not appropriate in a workplace. If you want to have such an e-mail address for your personal e-mail, you can establish a different e-mail account for that purpose.
- Use the subject line to tell the recipients of your e-mail what you are writing about. Leaving it blank or writing something generic, like "hi," can be dangerous, as someone might assume it is "spam" and delete it.
- The more formal and important the e-mail is, the more you should use proper letter etiquette: Address the recipient by last name, using a title such as "Dr.," "Professor," "Mr.," or "Ms.," especially if you are not well-acquainted or if there is some social distance between you. Be sure to include your name at the end of the e-mail, so the recipient knows who you are. Adding other contact information, such as your address and phone number, can also be helpful.
- Take time when composing an e-mail. The more important the subject, the longer you should take. E-mail should not be less professional than an office memo. Be concise without being brusque or leaving out important information. Use correct grammar and spelling, and correct your typos. Proofread your message before you send it, and think about whether the content says all you want it to.
- Do not write in all capital letters. Do not use excessive punctuation or no punctuation at all. Do not include emoticons or abbreviations (like TTYL and IMHO).
- Don't use the tab key to begin a new paragraph; skip a line instead.
- When sending attachments, be sure to mention in the body of your e-mail that you are doing so, and explain what the attached file contains. This can eliminate fear of viruses.

- When replying to another's e-mail, it can be helpful to use the reply option. This should automatically keep the sender's original subject line, with "Re:" in front. However, be careful that you are only e-mailing the people you want to. Note that some e-mail programs have an option to reply to all people who received the original e-mail. Keep the amount of quoted text in your reply to a minimum: rereading what one has already sent can be tedious.

- Respect the privacy of others and of yourself. E-mail is *never* completely private! Unless the sender indicates otherwise, treat e-mail messages as though they were meant for your eyes only. But don't assume that everyone else will do the same with e-mails that you send. If you have something confidential to say, it may be best to make an appointment with the person you want to talk to, so you don't have to put in writing something that may later embarrass or harm you.

- Be professional and respectful in your writing. Don't make personal attacks. Company e-mail systems are open to employer scrutiny, and e-mails can be forwarded, misdirected, hacked into, and so on. Once you hit the send button, you have no control over where your message goes.

- It can be helpful to postpone filling in the recipient's e-mail address until you are positive that your e-mail is complete and correct. Waiting can ensure you never accidentally send something weren't ready to, even if you hit the wrong button.

11

BASIC PRINCIPLES OF DOCUMENT DESIGN

CHAPTER OVERVIEW

After reading this chapter, you should be able to answer the following questions:

1. How does page layout contribute to a document's readability? What are some desirable features of page layout?
2. What is a typeface? What is meant by type weight? How is type size indicated?
3. What should you consider in choosing a font, a type weight, and a type size?
4. How do headings help indicate the structure of a document?
5. How are headings to be used in APA style? In Turabian style?

ENHANCING A DOCUMENT'S READABILITY

A document's readability is either enhanced or impeded by its visual design. Regardless of how eloquent your words are, if your document is visually daunting to the reader, it will be difficult to read. Research indicates that readers use a text's visual design in order to sum up its structure and make sense of the text itself (Huckin 1983; Redish, Battison, and Gold 1985). You should therefore design your documents to be structurally clear and visually easy to navigate. Elements of document design such as page layout, typography, and headings, when used effectively, will help the reader see the structure of your document, and understand and remember it with less effort. Word processing programs have many features that make it easy to create an effective design for most documents.

PAGE LAYOUT

A page that appears crowded distracts and burdens the reader.

The following paragraphs explain some of the document design principles that will improve the page layout of the documents you write.

Scan zones. The short headings arranged to the left of the text form a "scan zone." By using a zone like this for short, concise headings that describe the corresponding blocks of text, you make it easier for readers to scan your document and skip over the information they do not need. Scan zones are particularly suited for documents that are meant to be read quickly for specific information, documents such as guidelines, instructions, and resumes.

White space. White space is the space on a page that surrounds the text. White space, or the lack of it, shows relationships between items—it sets off one group from another. Whether you use a little or a lot, your goal should be to use white space for effect.

White space as an organizer of ideas. White space should also be used to show the organization and relationships within the text. When the spacing and location of the text follow a consistent pattern, they help the readers see a text's hierarchy and order of ideas. Use white space to separate groups of ideas. Indent your text appropriately to show where different topics or ideas begin and end. Separate sections with white space.

Lists. Listing a series of items vertically rather than as regular running text can often make a page more readable and the list items easier to remember. Lists should be set off by white space in order to draw the reader's attention. Be sure to keep all the elements of a list grammatically parallel.

Bullets and other graphic devices. Most word processing programs allow you to add bullets and other graphic devices such as carets, rules, and bars to your document:

- This is a bullet
- Δ   This is a caret

Bullets, carets, and other similar graphic devices can be helpful visual organizers, especially in lists where the items have no particular sequence. Numbered lists should be used when the items do have a particular order they should appear in, e.g., as steps in a process. Just because you can insert a bullet doesn't mean you always should. Excessive graphic devices can make a page very busy and visually overwhelming. A good rule to remember when using graphic devices is "less is more."

Many word processors allow you to insert small novelty graphics, sometimes called "wingdings" or "dingbats." (Here are some typical ones: ♣✍✗✄). You should keep your audience in mind when you decide whether or not to use wingdings or dingbats. For most academic and professional writing, they are inappropriate. However, they may be appropriate when you are writing for more familiar audiences and for less formal purposes.

TYPOGRAPHY

The term typography refers to the face, size, and weight of "type" or the letters printed on a page. The face, size, and weight of type are all design elements that, if used effectively, will enhance the readability of your document.

Fonts. Most computer word processors allow you to select from a large variety of typefaces, more accurately called fonts.

Serif vs. sans-serif fonts. There are two basic groups of fonts—serif fonts, which have extensions, or tiny lines on the edges of letters, and sans-serif fonts, which do not use extensions. Note the difference in these examples:

This is serif type. Times, Palatino, **New Century Schoolbook**, and `Courier` are all examples of serif type.

This is a sans-serif type. Arial, Helvetica, Gill Sans, Berlin, and AvantGarde are all examples of sans-serif type.

Some fonts are neither serif nor sans-serif. These fonts can be generally classified into two categories, script fonts and novelty fonts:

This is an example of a script font.
This is an example of a novelty font.

Use script and novelty fonts sparingly because they draw attention to themselves. You should stick to serif or sans-serif fonts for most academic and professional writing.

Follow these guidelines when selecting and using a font for your documents:

- **Use a serif font as your main font.** Because serif fonts create horizontal base lines, they help the eye move from one word to the next, making reading easier.

- **Use sans-serif fonts for titles and headings.** Because sans-serif fonts have predominantly vertical lines, they accentuate individual words, making them especially appropriate for titles and headings.
- **Select appropriate fonts for headings and text and stick to them.**

Capital letters. Avoid using all capital letters for regular text. Because we read in part by recognizing the shape of a word, capital letters are less legible than lowercase letters or mixed upper- and lowercase letters because they obscure the shape of the word. Words in all capitals are especially difficult to read if they are in a sans-serif font. Compare these two examples:

COMMERCIALS ARE NOW THE DOMINANT MEANS OF CANDIDATE COMMUNICATION IN TODAY'S POLITICAL RACES. VOTERS ARE NOW BOMBARDED WITH MILLIONS OF DOLLARS IN SPOT ADS DURING THE POLITICAL SEASON. THE 1990 ELECTIONS ALONE GENERATED $203 MILLION IN SPENDING ON ADS, ACCORDING TO AN ESTIMATE BY A BROADCASTING GROUP.

Commercials are now the dominant means of candidate communication in today's political races. Voters are now bombarded with millions of dollars in spot ads during the political season. The 1990 elections alone generated $203 million in spending on ads, according to an estimate by a broadcasting group.

The first example, written in all capitals, is more difficult to read than the second example, which varies upper- and lowercase letters.

Type size. Most word processors offer a wide range of type sizes—called "point sizes"—to choose from. The larger a type's point size, the larger the type is. Note these various type sizes:

This is Times 6-point.

This is Times 9-point.

This is Times 12-point.

This is Times 18-point.

This is Times 32-point.

For regular text, you should use a 9- to 12-point type size—point sizes lower than 8 are very difficult to read and are best suited for informal documents. Point sizes larger than 12 are better suited for titles and headings.

Type weight. As a general rule, use medium-weight fonts for regular text. **Very light and very heavy fonts (such as the boldface used for this sentence) are tiring to read.** However, you may want to use boldface type to emphasize words or short passages of text. Research shows that readers notice changes in type weight more readily than they notice changes in font (Spencer, Reynolds, and Coe 1973).

VISUAL CUES TO TEXT STRUCTURE

HEADINGS

Headings serve as the "road map" to your document—they help readers scan the document quickly to locate information and they help readers develop a framework within which they can more easily understand and remember the text.

Heading content. Researchers have found that headings that use complete and specific phrasing, especially full statements or questions, are particularly effective in making a text easier to read (Hartley, Morris, and Trueman 1981). Compare the headings from two outlines in Figures 11-1 and 11-2.

Notice how informative and useful the headings in 11-2 are compared to 11-1. The headings in 11-2 are effective because they are descriptive and specific rather than general and vague—for the most part, they contain a verb rather than a single noun or short noun string. They can be read apart from the text and still make sense.

Heading design. Design your headings so that your document's hierarchy of information is visually distinguishable. In other words, design your headings so that the reader can tell if a particular heading pertains to the paper in general, a large section of text, or a small portion of text. Use distinguishing elements consistently so that, at any point in the text, the reader knows which level a particular heading belongs to.

You can distinguish the level of a heading by changing various type features.

You can vary the type size:

Very Large Type

Large Type

Regular type

FIGURE 11-1. An outline made from vague, generic headings

I.   Introduction
II. History
III. The Pathological Perspective
     A. Definition
     B. Techniques
IV. The Cultural Perspective
     A. Definition
     B. Reforms
V.   Conclusion

FIGURE 11-2. An outline made from specific, informative headings

I.   Introduction
II. Early Deaf History in America
     A. Thomas Gallaudet: American Pioneer in Deaf Education
     B. American Sign Language: A Hybrid of European and Indigenous
         Sign Languages
     C. Founding of Gallaudet University
     D. 1817–1880: The "Golden Age" of the Deaf
III. The Tendency to Consider Deafness a Disease
     A. The "Pathological" Perspective Defined
     B. 1880–1960: The Pathological Perspective Prevails
     C. Recent Methods of "Treating" Deafness
         1. Oralism: Restoring the Deaf to Society
         2. Imposing English Grammar on Sign Language
IV. An Alternative to the Pathological Perspective: Viewing the Deaf as a
     Culture
     A. The Cultural Perspective Defined
     B. How Hearing Societies Can Adopt the Cultural Perspective
         1. Treating American Sign Language as a Unique Language
         2. Celebrating the Unique Values of the Deaf Community
         3. Becoming Aware of the Deaf Community's Unique Social
             Conventions
         4. Celebrating the Deaf Community's Literature and Traditions
V.   Conclusion

You can vary the type weight:

Bold-face type

Medium-weight type

You can vary the capitalization:

In This Heading, the First Letter of Each Important Word is Capitalized

In this heading only the first letter is capitalized

You can underline text or put it in italics:

<u>This is an underlined heading</u>

This heading is in italics

You can combine several of these elements:

<u>**This Heading is in Initial Capitals, is Underlined, and is in Boldface Type**</u>

Or you can use a different font altogether.

This heading is in a sans-serif font

The main text is in a serif font

You can also vary the spacing on the page. You can center a title or heading:

This Heading is Centered

The text starts here and continues. . . .

You can keep a heading flush with the left margin:

This heading is flush left

The text starts here and continues. It keeps going in this example so you can see how it would look. . . .

You can indent the heading above the text:

> **This heading is indented above the text**
>
> The text starts here and continues. These lines of text will help you see how this kind of heading would look. . . .

Or you can indent the heading and place the text adjacent to it:

> **This heading is indented and next to text.** The text continues from here and wraps down to additional lines. . . .

You can also use a rule to distinguish a heading:

> ## This Heading is Separated from the Text with a Rule
>
> The text starts here and continues . . .

Notice how font, size, and weight are used to show different levels of headings. Larger point sizes and bold-faced type are used for major headings, while italics and medium-weight type are used for minor headings.

Additional advice regarding headings. There are a few more things to remember regarding headings: unless your style guide says otherwise, limit the number of heading levels to four or less. If you use more than four levels of headings, your document can become confusing and difficult to read. Also, remember that readers will expect headings in larger point sizes to be more important than headings in smaller ones. And they will expect a heading in all capitals to be more important than a heading in mixed- or lowercase type. Finally, don't leave a heading at the bottom of a page if the text starts on the following page. You should have at least one line of text accompany a heading.

HEADINGS AND PROFESSIONAL STYLE GUIDES

If your document must adhere to a particular style guide, such as APA or Turabian, you should follow its prescriptions for headings.

LEVEL 5 HEADINGS ARE CENTERED IN UPPERCASE

Level 1 Headings are Centered in Uppercase and Lowercase

Level 2 Headings are Centered, Uppercase and Lowercase, and Underlined

Level 3 Headings are Flush Left, Uppercase and Lowercase, and Underlined

      Level 4 headings are indented to begin the paragraph, lowercase, and underlined, and they end with a period.

Not every document you write will require all five levels of headings. APA offers the following guidelines for selecting level formats when you use fewer than five heading levels:

> *One level.* When you only have one level of headings, use the format for Level 1 headings described above.
>
> *Two levels.* When your document has two levels of headings, use Level 1 and Level 3 heading formats.
>
> *Three levels.* For three levels of headings, use Level 1, Level 3, and Level 4 heading formats.
>
> *Four levels.* When you have four levels of headings, use the heading formats for Levels 1 through 4.
>
> *Five levels.* When you have five levels of headings, use Level 5 format for broadest heading, then Levels 1 through 4.

Like APA, Turabian (1996) suggests that no more than five levels of headings be used. According to Turabian, the following formats may be used for each of the five levels.

Level 1 Headings are in Boldface, Italicized, or Underlined, Centered, and Capitalized Headline Style

Level 2 Headings are in Text Type, Centered, and Capitalized Headline Style

Level 3 Headings are in Boldface, Italicized, or Underlined, Flush Left, and Capitalized Headline Style.

Level 4 headings are in text type, flush left, and capitalized sentence style.

   Level 5 headings are in boldface, italicized, and/or underlined, are indented to begin a paragraph, and are capitalized sentence style with a period at the end.

If you don't need five levels of headings, Turabian suggests that you select the heading formats you prefer from those shown above, always making sure that you use them in descending order.

There is more to document design than the brief pointers covered in this chapter, but these relatively simple guidelines are ones you can implement with most word processing programs. Using these principles will make the documents you create for school and on the job more readable.

REFERENCES

Gregory, M. and E. C. Poulton. 1975. Even versus uneven right-hand margins and the rate of comprehension in reading. *Applied Ergonomics* 6.

Hartley, J. and P. Burnhill. 1971. Experiments with unjustified text. *Visible Language* 5, 265–278.

Hartley, J., P. Morris, & M. Trueman. 1981. Headings in text. *Remedial Education* 15, 5–6.

Huckin, Thomas N. 1983. A cognitive approach to readability. In *New Essays in Technical and Scientific Communication: Research, Theory, and Practice*, eds. Paul V. Anderson, R. John Brockmann, and Carolyn R. Miller, 90–101. Farmingdale, NY: Baywood.

Redish, Janice C., Robin M. Battison, and Edward S. Gold. 1985. Making information accessible to readers. In *Writing in Nonacademic Settings*, eds. Lee Odell and Dixie Goswami, 129–53. New York: Guilford.

Spencer, H., L. Reynolds, & B. Coe. 1973. *A comparison of the effectiveness of selected typographic variations*. Readability of Print Research Unit, London: Royal College of Art.

Turabian, Kate. 1996. *A manual for writers of term papers, theses, and dissertations*. 6th ed. Chicago: University of Chicago Press.

12

GRAPHICS

CHAPTER OVERVIEW

After reading this chapter, you should be able to answer the following questions:

1. In what sense can graphics be a kind of rhetoric?
2. What are tables? What are figures?
3. What kinds of figures might you include in a written report?
4. Where do you position graphics in a paper? How do you direct the reader to look at them?
5. How should tables and figures be numbered and labeled?
6. What are some of the ethical issues associated with using graphics?

GRAPHICS AS RHETORIC

Graphics are tables and figures that you can add to your writing to clarify and illustrate the ideas or facts you are writing about. *Tables* are rows and columns of data—words or numbers or both—that display the data in a small space so that it is easy for the reader to see relationships among various parts of the entire set of data. *Figures* are all other illustrations that are not tables. Figures include photographs, line drawings, maps, diagrams, flowcharts, and various kinds of graphs—line graphs, circle graphs, and bar graphs (also called column graphs). In this chapter you will learn principles for creating clear, appropriate tables and figures and for integrating them into the texts that you write so that your writing is rhetorically effective.

It may seem that graphics are always so straightforward and neutral that they have no persuasive dimension, hence do not belong to the study of rhetoric. If you recall the definition of rhetoric used in Chapter 1, you may remember this part of it:

> Rhetoric is using words and other symbols skillfully to articulate and advocate your beliefs about something you assume to be true, addressing an audience you want to persuade to assent to your beliefs by choice, not by coercion, and possibly to cooperate with you. . . .

Well-made graphics use symbols and design principles skillfully to appeal to the visual sense, enhancing and clarifying a message, making it more persuasive than it might otherwise be. Poorly designed, badly integrated, or incomplete graphics can detract from the effectiveness of a message because they call into question the writer's knowledge. Misleading graphics cast doubt on the writer's trustworthiness, detracting from the ethical appeal of the message.

In today's world, visual rhetoric is very important. Consider the advertisements you see each day on television and billboards or in newspapers and magazines. The ad-makers work very hard to create images and words that will catch your attention and stay in your memory, subtly or not so subtly persuading you to buy a product or try a service. It is fairly easy to see that graphics (usually photographs) in advertising are a form of rhetoric. Unlike academic and professional rhetoric, advertising rhetoric usually relies heavily on appeals to emotion. It sometimes appeals to other aspects of human nature as well, such as our senses and our basic drives and appetites.

As a consumer bombarded daily with advertising rhetoric, you must be alert to the kinds of hidden appeals embedded in the words and images of ads so that you can evaluate their messages rationally and avoid being unconsciously manipulated by this kind of rhetoric. Similarly, as a reader of social science research, you need to evaluate graphics for their clarity, completeness, and appropriateness of design. Probably very few social scientists set out to manipulate their audiences, but they may inadvertently make their writing less effective and credible than it could be by not creating understandable and reliable graphics.

As a student of the social sciences, you should not only learn how to read and judge graphics knowledgeably; you should also be able to create them so that you can display complex data in a concise, readable form. Because graphics are becoming much easier to create with various kinds of computer software, it will be to your advantage to learn to use one or more graphics programs. However, some features of the available software programs are not based on sound communication and design principles, so you need to be aware of the potential flaws and ethical pitfalls in creating graphics with computers—such as needless third dimensions in bar graphs or cute but empty illustrations on tables and graphs. You shouldn't forsake simplicity and clarity for what graphic designer Edward Tufte calls "chartjunk" simply because a computer program allows you to create it. More will be said about chartjunk and the ethics of creating graphics at the end of this chapter.

TABLES

Tables are efficient, compact summaries of large data sets presented in rows and columns. The pattern formed by the rows and columns resembles a grid, even when the rows and columns do not have visible lines subdividing the grid into cells. Whether the lines are there or not, however, it is helpful to think of a table as containing a cell for each item of information that you want to display. Suppose, for example, that you conduct a survey of undergraduate students' reasons for reading the daily campus newspaper. You identify four primary reasons why students read the newspaper, as well as a few miscellaneous reasons you can characterize as "other." So you identify five reasons in all. You also learn that the percentage of students giving each reason varies with year in college—that is, from the freshman to the senior year.

To display these twenty items of data, you would need a 4 x 5 grid. You could create four columns to display the reasons and four rows to display the years in college; the intersection of these rows and columns would create sixteen cells. However, in order for a reader to know what the cells represent, you would also need another row to label the columns and an extra column to label the rows, so you would have to make a 5 x 6 grid. Your table might look like the one in Table 12-1.

This table permits your audience to read the data horizontally to see what the most important and least important reasons are for each group of students; it also enables your audience to read vertically to see how the importance of a particular reason changes as the average student progresses through college. The table would also permit the reader to quickly compare any two items of information. Besides helping the reader, this table would help you as the writer to draw conclusions about the significance of the survey findings and interpret them. What trends do you notice in the data? What plausible explanations for these trends can you give?

TABLE 12-1. A Simple Table

Students' Reasons for Reading the Campus Newspaper

	Read world and national news	Learn about campus events	Read advertisements	Read about sports	Other Reasons
Freshman	11%	70%	9%	9%	1%
Sophomore	15%	64%	11%	8%	2%
Junior	36%	33%	17%	11%	3%
Senior	45%	10%	30%	10%	5%

TABLE 12-2. A Table Made of Words

Comparison of Quantitative and Qualitative Methods

	Types	Advantages	Limitations
Quantitative methods	Experiments Surveys	Possibility of large sample size Generalizability and breadth High degree of control	Loss of particularity Possibly high costs
Qualitative methods	Interviews Observations Documents	Rich data Particularity and depth Large scope for interpretation	Low generalizability Overwhelming data Time consumption

Imagine how much more difficult it would be for a reader to make comparisons or notice trends if the data in Table 12-1 were to be explained in paragraph form. You would have to write a very long and complex paragraph to present all of this information, and the paragraph would be much more time-consuming and tiresome to read than the table. It would be difficult for the reader to pick out any two items of information for comparison. You can strengthen the credibility of your interpretations if they are based on data that are easy to find, to read, and to understand.

Tables usually present numbers, but they can also consist of words. Table 12-2 (reproduced from Chapter 3) compares the advantages and disadvantages of quantitative and qualitative research methods. It presents a handy summary of information that took several paragraphs to explain.

You can create simple tables with word processing programs. Many of them have special functions to help you create tables. Even without a special tables function, however, it is not difficult to align data in columns and rows simply by setting up tabs or columns with your word processing program. You can also use computer spreadsheets into which you can enter data and then convert the data from the spreadsheet into a table.

FIGURES

As noted above, figures are all graphics that are not tables. (In some fields, these graphics might also go by the name "illustration," "exhibit," "chart," or even "visual." In most social science journals, however, these graphics are usually called figures.) In the next few pages, some of the most common types of figures are described and illustrated, and guidelines are provided for creating these kinds of graphics.

PHOTOGRAPHS

A photograph is an especially useful kind of figure when you are writing about a person—perhaps a famous one—or place and you want the reader to be able to see what the person or place actually looks like. Photographs are also helpful when you are writing about an object or event and it is important to give a realistic and detailed image of it, rather than the abstract, less concrete image provided by a sketch. They can be enlarged to show more detail. Photos can also be cropped to eliminate irrelevant parts of a picture. Because photographs reproduce every detail visible to the camera, however, they may cause the reader to get caught up in the little things and perhaps lose focus on the most important features of the illustration. Also, because photographs are more difficult and expensive to reproduce than drawings, you may need to limit their use.

If you decide that a photo is the best kind of illustration for a particular text, original photos must be of a high quality with high contrast between light and dark to provide the best reproductions. You will need to be skillful with a camera or hire someone to produce original photos. If you use a copyrighted photo, you will have to acknowledge the photographer and the copyright holder in the caption. You will likely have to pay a fee to others for permission to use their photos.

LINE DRAWINGS

Line drawings are simple sketches that eliminate much of the detail included in photos for the sake of simplifying and emphasizing the most important features of the illustration. Figure 12-1 is a line drawing of an archeological dig site showing the types of objects found at each level of the site excavated.

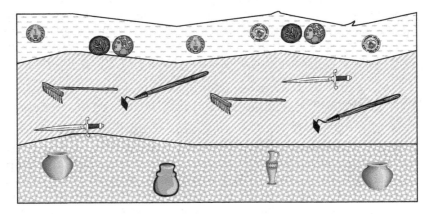

FIGURE 12-1. A Line Drawing

Line drawings to illustrate something like a dig site may be a more rhetorically effective choice than photographs because the simplicity of the drawing allows the writer to abstract from the detail that would be provided in a photo in order to emphasize the critical features of the site. A drawing imposes an interpretation on the raw physical data, so it may be more persuasive to the reader.

If, in your research, you find that line drawings would be the best choice to illustrate your main points, you might consider employing an artist to create the drawings if you don't feel competent to make them yourself, drawing freehand. However, using computer software that is readily available, you should, with some practice, be able to create effective drawings of your own.

MAPS

A map is a type of line drawing because it leaves out a lot of detail that could be included in order to simplify matters and to illustrate the writer's point. For example, a road map usually doesn't include the varying elevations of the terrain that the roads cross. A contour map, however, focuses on elevations and often leaves out roads. Maps such as these, which represent geographic realities, usually include a scale showing how much real distance is represented by each unit of distance (such as an inch or centimeter) on the map. These maps may also include legends (explained later in this chapter) indicating what the various symbols on the map stand for. For example, the legend might show that various kinds of lines represent interstate highways, state highways, improved roads, and unimproved roads.

Maps can also be used as ways of making points about political, economic, or social realities. For example, a simple map of the United States outlining the boundaries of the states is a favorite way used by newspapers and magazines for making various kinds of comparisons among the 50 states. By shading in the states that have capital punishment, for example, a writer can help the reader see at a glance how many and which states have such laws on the books. Figure 12-2 shows the number of interviews Christian Smith and his associates conducted in each state and where for the National Study of Youth and Religion.

DIAGRAMS AND FLOWCHARTS

A diagram is a drawing that simplifies a complex object or concept. Frequently diagrams represent abstract ideas or relationships, such as parts of a theory or a conceptual model. They may consist of both words and graphical elements such as lines, circles, boxes, arrows, etc. A particular kind of diagram is a flowchart, which generally depicts a process or the possible steps in an operation. Diagrams and flowcharts are excellent ways of summarizing visually the main points you make in words, so that the reader has a handy way to remember

FIGURE 12-2. A Map

concepts and how they are related to each other. The diagram in Figure 12-3 is from Kemarie Campbell's paper on causes of obesity in the US. This diagram shows the dieter's dilemma, or the cycle of restrained eating followed by cravings and loss of control.

GRAPHS

Graphs are special kinds of figures that allow you to display the relationships between numerical and categorical variables for easy comprehension and comparison. There are three kinds of commonly used graphs: line graphs, bar graphs, circle graphs.

Line graphs. Line graphs show the continuous relationship between at least two variables. The two variables are represented as points in a space defined by two axes—an *x*-axis (horizontal) and a *y*-axis (vertical)—each of which has been divided into meaningful increments. To show the continuous relationship between the two variables, you can draw a line from one point to the next, thus showing the upward and downward trends in the relationship between the variables. For example, the fluctuations of a particular stock price over a period of months can be clearly represented by a line graph, as shown in

Reprinted from *Soul Searching: The Religious and Spiritual Lives of American Teenagers* (2005), Oxford University Press.

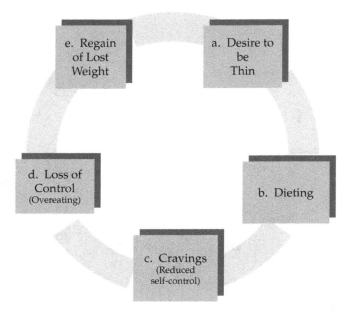

FIGURE 12-3. A Diagram

Figure 12-4. The *x*-axis names the months in a six-month period; the *y*-axis shows the prices per share of the stock. The maker of this graph simply plotted a point to represent the price for the stock each month and then connected the points to make a line showing the overall trend.

More than one line can be plotted on a particular line graph. For example, the line graph in Figure 12-4 could have a second line showing the price fluctuation of a different stock over the same period of time. The second line could be drawn as a broken or a dotted line to differentiate it from the first one. Still more lines could be added as long as each could be clearly distinguished from the others. However, too many lines that cross each other at numerous points would clutter the graph and make it confusing and difficult to read.

Bar (column) graphs. Like a line graph, a bar graph also plots the relationship between at least two variables by using two clearly labeled and subdivided axes. The difference is that a bar graph is used when the independent variable is categorical, rather than numerical. The data are represented as discrete units, rather than as continuous, the way they are in a line graph. Thus, one axis is not a numbered scale; instead, it is divided into categories of data, and each bar on the graph represent a different amount or number in a particular category. Using bars with different shading or cross-hatching, you can even compare data for different groups within each category.

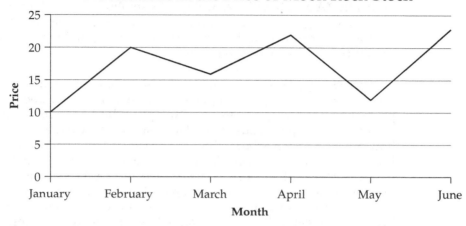

FIGURE 12-4. A Line Graph

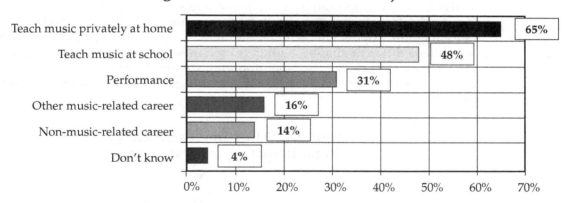

FIGURE 12-5. A Bar Graph

For example, in the bar graph in Figure 12-5 from a student paper on the professional and educational goals of music majors, the y-axis shows categories of career goals chosen by participants in the survey. The x-axis shows the total percentage of the respondents that chose each career goal.

Another important thing to notice about the bar graph in Figure 12-5 is that each bar is labeled at its end with the exact percentage of respondents who chose each category. Even though the x-axis is divided into increments of ten percent, it is important to let the reader know the exact figure in any category. The standard way to do this is to write the exact figure on the bar or at the end of the bar. Note also that the bars in a bar graph can run either horizontally or vertically. (A graph with vertical bars is sometimes called a column graph.) In the case of Figure 12-5, horizontal bars were a good choice so that the labels for the categories could be written horizontally, making them easier to read than if they were written vertically.

Circle graphs. Circle graphs are also called "pie charts" because they are divided into wedges just as a pie is. They are particularly good for representing percentages and proportions. For example, a budget is commonly represented with a circle graph because the relative size of the wedges makes it easy to see how much money has been allotted to each budget category. Usually, the circle is considered to be like a clock face, and the wedges are put in descending order of size starting at 12 o'clock. Sometimes, however, the convention of descending order is not followed in order to keep wedges that are similar close to each other.

Like a line or bar graph, a circle graph can present too much data and become confusing. If a circle graph has very many wedges, several of the wedges are likely to be very small, and it will become more difficult for a reader to see the relative differences in size. It is also difficult to label very small wedges of a circle graph, so a bar graph might be a better choice when a lot of categories are to be compared. However, if the pie will be cut into only a few wedges, a circle graph can be a good choice to show the divisions of a whole. Figure 12-6 is a simple circle graph from the same student paper showing the percentage of respondents who chose three different answers to a question. Note that a different kind of shading is used in each wedge to help distinguish the wedges and help you see the proportions more clearly. Note also that the responses and the percentages choosing that response are written just outside each of the wedges.

Figure 4. "How interested are you in participating in a career fair?"
not interested (11%)
very interested (43%)
somewhat interested (46%)

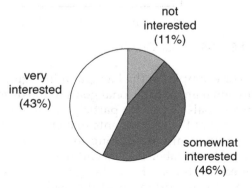

FIGURE 12-6. A Circle Graph

POSITIONING AND LABELING GRAPHICS

Position Graphics for Easy Viewing

Once you have decided what kinds of graphics will best illustrate your verbal message, next you must determine where to put the graphics in the text. If graphics are meant to illustrate and clarify a verbal text, it is important to place them as close to the relevant text as you possibly can—on the same or the following page, so that the reader can easily pause while reading to glance at or study the graphic. Sometimes graphics can be made small enough that the text can run in a narrow column right next to the graphic. Sometimes graphics are so big that they must cover two pages or even be printed on extra large paper that can be folded into the document and then unfolded when the reader is ready to look at them. Occasionally, however, graphics present information that is interesting and relevant, but not critical for the reader to see while reading the text. In this case, graphics can be placed in an appendix to the document for readers to look at or not, as they choose.

Number Graphics for Easy Reference

Although positioning a graphic in the most advantageous place is an important way to help the reader, position by itself is not enough to make reference to the graphic convenient. Each graphic also needs a number so that you can refer to it without having to write something clumsy like "the bar graph showing the means for each year at the top of page 4" or "the table on page 2 that compares men's and women's responses." Usually tables and figures are numbered separately from each other. So if you created a document that had two tables and three figures, they would be called Table 1 and Table 2, and Figure 1, Figure 2, and Figure 3 respectively.

Giving each graphic a number helps you refer to it conveniently as often as you need to. In the text of your paper, you can refer directly to a graphic by writing something like this: "As Table 1 shows, students in the experimental treatment scored significantly higher on the post-test." Or you can refer more indirectly, using parentheses: "Investments rose as inflation declined (see Figure 1)." But it is important to refer to your graphics and to discuss their significance. Don't simply put them in your paper and expect your reader to figure out why they are there and what they show.

Give Graphics Descriptive Captions

Besides numbering your graphics, you should add a descriptive caption that allows a reader who is skimming your document to understand what kind of information the graphic displays without having to read the verbal text. Rather than make your captions vague (e.g., "Comparisons") or cute (e.g., "Sexist Sentencing"), make them long enough to be informative. For example, don't be reluctant to write a long, specific and detailed caption such as the following: "Comparison of Prison Sentences for Males and Females Convicted of the Same Kinds of Crimes."

LABEL PARTS OF TABLES AND FIGURES

Besides positioning, numbering, and labeling graphics, you will have to add other information to make clear what kind of information each part of each graphic shows. For tables, you will have to label the columns and rows, and you may have to add more information in notes, depending on your purpose and audience needs. For drawings, diagrams, and flow charts, you may need to label individual parts. For line and bar graphs, you have to label the axes; for circle graphs, you have to label the wedges. For all of these, you may need to add a legend. Each of these features is explained and illustrated below.

Labeling parts of tables. In addition to a number and a caption, a table needs other information, depending on how complicated the depicted information is. Each column and each row needs a heading so that a reader can tell what particular information is given in each cell. Notice the various kinds of headings and subheadings used in Table 12-3.

As you can see from Table 12-3, a table can have footnotes besides column and row headings and subheadings. A table can also have other information

TABLE 12-3. A Complex Table

Comparison of Male and Female Professors' Job Satisfaction and Job Performance Ratings

Rank	Mean Job Satisfaction Rating[a]		Mean Job Performance Rating by Chair[a]		Mean Self-Performance Rating[a]	
	Male[b]	Female[c]	Male	Female	Male	Female
Assistant Professor	4.3	3.5	4.5	5.3	5.0	4.3
Associate Professor	5.2	4.3	6.0	6.0	5.7	5.4
Professor	6.5	5.4	5.6	5.6	6.7	5.5

[a] All rankings are based on a 7-point scale, where 7 is greatest.
[b] $n = 46$.
[c] $n = 24$.

printed immediately above or under it to help the reader understand the context of the data.

Labeling parts of graphs. On a circle graph, you must make clear what each wedge stands for. You can do this by writing directly on the wedge what it represents. If the wedge is too small, you can write the description outside the circle and draw a line to the wedge the description stands for, as Figure 12-7 shows.

Line graphs and bar graphs plot data along two axes, the *y*-axis (vertical) and the *x*-axis (horizontal). Usually, numerical values are shown on the *y*-axis and any other variable (such as time or a category) on the *x*-axis; however, this convention can be reversed, as it is in Figure 12-5. Remember that your reader needs to know what information you are showing on each axis, so clearly label each one, as Figure 12-8 shows. Figure 12-8 also shows the use of a *legend*. Legends are used when figures present several kinds of data on one grid; the legend helps the reader understand the figure by showing what different kinds of lines, shading, or cross-hatching stand for. For example, if you had a bar graph with several different bars in each category, you could create a legend that helps the reader understand what each bar represents. Figure 12-8 shows how a legend can be incorporated.

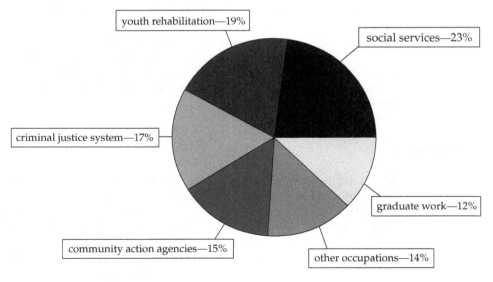

FIGURE 12-7. A Labeled Circle Graph

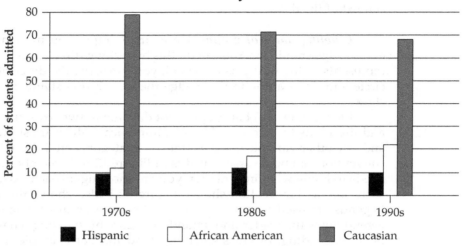

FIGURE 12-8. A Bar Graph with a Legend

ETHICAL ISSUES IN USING GRAPHICS

As you learned in Chapter 1, rhetoric can be used for good or ill. Your ethical stance as a writer will be evident in the choices you make in composing and presenting information to your readers, including how you present graphical information. With graphics there are basically three areas of concern: plagiarism; omitting information or not following reasonable conventions for representing variations in the data; and unfairly manipulating the impression the graphic makes on the reader by using chartjunk or distorting or cluttering the design of the graphic.

PLAGIARISM

Much of the time, graphics in your writing will present original data that you have gathered in your own research. However, graphics could present information that you have borrowed from other people's research and adapted to display in graphic form. Or they could be reproductions of graphics someone else made, which you have recreated, photocopied, or electronically scanned to use in your own documents. In either of the latter two cases—borrowed information or adapted graphics—you would need to give credit to the original source in your paper, just as you would for a quotation, summary, or paraphrase of words you have borrowed. Failing to cite the source of graphical data would be a form of plagiarism. If you create a graphic out of adapted information or reproduce a graphic, the easiest way to attribute it to the source is to put a credit line in small type underneath the graphic. You would also cite the source in the reference list of your paper.

OMITTING OR MISREPRESENTING VARIATIONS IN THE DATA

Graphics can be misleading, and therefore unethical, when they don't show all the pertinent data or they misrepresent the data, making something appear to be the case that isn't actually so. One way that the maker of a graphic might misrepresent is by using an inappropriate scale on the y-axis of a line graph or bar graph or by changing the unit of division in the scale at some point. For example, notice that in Figure 12-9, at first it appears that campus rapes have risen sharply in one year. But then notice the unit of division on the y-axis.

Figure 12-9 uses an inappropriate scale on the y-axis, decimal figures ascending in increments of two-tenths. But it makes no sense to think of two-tenths of a rape. In actuality, there has been one rape in a three-year period, but this graph might at first lead a reader to believe there has been a startling jump. While no one wants to minimize the seriousness of even one rape on any campus, it is important to give readers an accurate rather than misleading depiction of any statistical data.

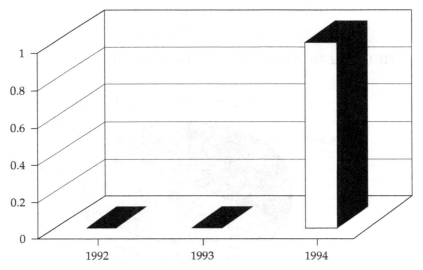

FIGURE 12-9. A Misleading Graph

DISTORTING OR CLUTTERING THE DESIGN

Graphics can also border on unethical if they distort the impression the reader gets from the actual design. There are two common sources for this kind of problem: (1) using three-dimensional bars on a bar graph (as in Figure 12-9) or adding a third dimension to a circle graph can distort the data by changing the viewers' perspective of the graph and causing them to misunderstand the comparative size of the bars or wedges; (2) adding "chartjunk"—cute but unnecessary illustrations, objects, or icons to a graph either draws the viewer's attention away from the real information the graphic has to convey or makes it difficult to find the information. Following are two illustrations that show distortion and clutter. Figure 12-10 distorts by using a needless third dimension in the bars, making it more difficult to compare the heights of the bars. Figure 12-11 shows

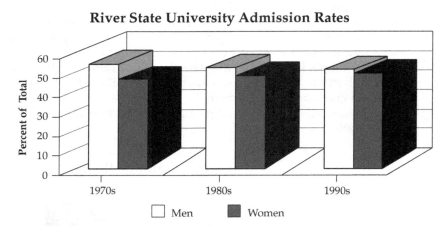

FIGURE 12-10. A Distorted Three-Dimensional Bar Graph

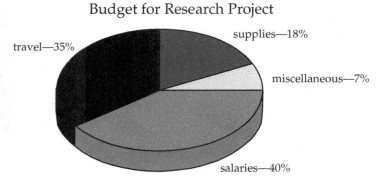

FIGURE 12-11. A Distorted Three-Dimensional Circle Graph

how adding a third dimension to a pie chart makes the wedges in the foreground look bigger than they are.

Figure 12-12 draws attention away from the important information by using chartjunk, perhaps in an attempt to make the chart more entertaining or

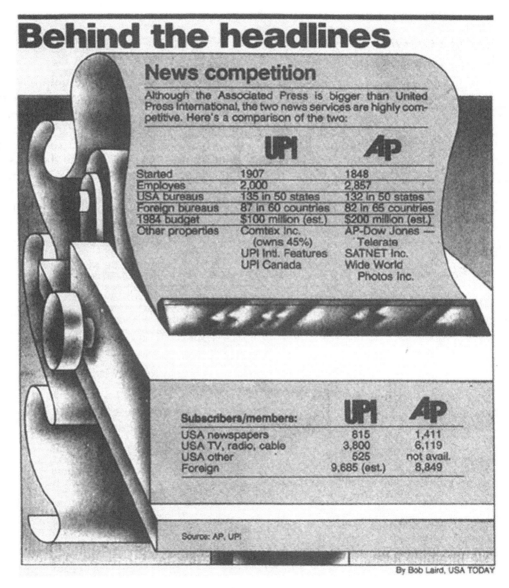

FIGURE 12-12. An Example of Chartjunk

picturesque. When you finally locate the basic information the chart conveys, however, you may feel that the maker of the chart has overwhelmed the data by unnecessarily giving prominence to something that is meant to be a clever illustration. By cluttering the chart, the designer causes you to spend more time searching for and interpreting the basic information.

CONCLUSION

You will frequently see graphics in newspapers and popular magazines that violate the principles this chapter espouses. One reason may be that untrained designers create the graphics to add color and entertainment to an article. Another reason is that many computer programs for graphics actually invite the user to clutter figures with junk, add needless third dimensions, or display information in a type of graph that isn't suited for the data. As you read professional journals in your field, however, you will notice that graphics are usually simpler and clearer than in popular periodicals. You are well advised to study the graphics of professional publications so that you can become both a wise consumer and producer of informative figures and tables.

REFERENCE

Tufte, Edward. 1990. *Envisioning information.* Cheshire, CN: Graphics Press.

13

ORAL PRESENTATIONS

CHAPTER OVERVIEW

After reading this chapter, you should be able to answer the following questions:

1. How do you evaluate the rhetorical situation when you have to give a speech?
2. What should the opening of a speech do? How can you get the audience's attention?
3. How does speaking differ from writing? What are the implications of the difference for the way you should organize the middle of a speech?
4. What should the ending of an oral presentation do?
5. What are the advantages and disadvantages of various kinds of visual aids?
6. What factors are important to remember in the delivery of an oral presentation?

THE TRADITION OF ORAL RHETORIC

As you learned in the opening chapter of this book, the ancient study of rhetoric focused on analyzing and teaching the art of public speaking. Two of the divisions of classical rhetoric—memory and delivery—taught students mnemonic devices to help them memorize their speeches and the art of using just the right stance, gestures, and voice inflections to make their words emphatic and memorable. In the eighteenth and early nineteenth centuries, the main goal in teaching rhetoric at the university was to produce skilled orators who could take their place in society as ministers, lawyers, judges, legislators, doctors, and professors. The ability to speak eloquently and persuasively was considered a prime requirement for these professions and was the hallmark of an educated man (women did not regularly have access to higher education until the twentieth century). Some of the rituals that are still a part of traditional university life—debates, valedictory addresses, and oral exams—are a result of the strong emphasis on rhetorical training from the Middle Ages until well into the nineteenth century.

Being an effective, persuasive speaker is still vital for success in most avenues of professional life, just as it is for any citizen interested in affecting the course of local government. But in this century, what little rhetorical instruction students receive is usually limited to writing (and then only one or two courses). Courses in public speaking are still taught at most universities and colleges, but they are often no longer required. As a result, it is possible to graduate from college now without having formally studied and practiced the art of oral rhetoric. This is unfortunate because it is valuable to have the ability to get people to listen to you, to take your ideas seriously, and even to join you in action. While this chapter can't take the place of a full course in public speaking, it can offer some pointers that should be useful in your future—whether you present research findings at the meetings of professional organizations, go to a city council meeting to influence the local zoning ordinances, or make presentations to your supervisor or your subordinates on the job. You will learn how to evaluate each rhetorical situation, organize your presentation, use resources wisely, and plan and rehearse your delivery.

EVALUATING THE RHETORICAL SITUATION

Just as you do when you write, the first thing you should do when planning an oral presentation is evaluate your rhetorical situation: What is your purpose? Who is your audience? What do you intend to talk about? Whether you are writing or speaking, these are questions you must always answer when composing a text.

DEFINING YOUR PURPOSE

Your general purposes in any oral presentation will usually be to inform and persuade—though not always in equal measure. Sometimes your purpose may be to entertain (e.g., when serving as master of ceremonies) or respond appropriately on a ceremonial occasion (e.g., when receiving an award, proposing a toast, giving a eulogy). In addition to identifying your general purposes, you also need to define your immediate purpose or goal for the particular speech you are planning. For example, suppose you were presenting your research findings about a new behavior modification therapy to a group of peers. You could formulate your immediate purpose as follows:

> To inform my colleagues about the theory and practice of therapy X and persuade them that it is effective in dealing with people who display behavior Y.

By defining your immediate goal as precisely as you can, you are better able to make decisions about what information and evidence to include in your presentation and how to arrange its parts.

SIZING UP YOUR AUDIENCE

You can hardly think about your immediate purpose without simultaneously thinking about your audience. Here are some questions that will help you decide how to achieve your purpose with a given audience:

- Who are my listeners?
- What do they already know about the subject?
- What position, if any, have they already taken on the subject? Are they likely to be skeptical, favorable, or neutral to my point of view?
- What do they already know about me and how do they feel about me?
- What relationship do they have to me? Are they my peers, my supervisors, my students, my subordinates?

As you can see from these questions, there are many variables to consider as you plan how to address your audience. For example, if your audience knows you already and knows your background, it will not be necessary to have someone introduce you and explain your credentials—or to work that into your talk if no introduction is to be given. If the audience knows little about your subject, you will have to think carefully about ways to give them a quick, basic understanding of it. If the audience already knows something about your subject, but is already inclined to disagree with you about it, you must plan ways to overcome their resistance. And if the audience members are your superiors and have the power to approve your ideas or grant money for a proposal, you must remember their need to be fully informed and to explore all the ramifications of the decisions they might make. You need to anticipate their concerns and be prepared to answer their questions.

ASSESSING THE CONTEXT AND ENVIRONMENT

As you define your immediate purpose and size up your audience, you should also assess the context and environment in which they will they be listening to you. Will you make your presentation to a class? During a board meeting? After dinner? At the end of a two-day conference? How many people will be there? What sort of mental and physical state are they likely to be in? How many minutes will you have to speak? What will the room be like in which you speak? Will it be a small classroom, a large auditorium, or a hotel conference room?

Will you be standing at a podium or seated with your audience around a table? To answer questions such as these, try to learn as much as you can about the context and environment for your presentation, as they will certainly affect the strategy you will want to use. (More will be said later about how to plan for the environment.)

ORGANIZING YOUR PRESENTATION

After you have considered the above aspects of the rhetorical situation, you can begin planning what to include in your presentation and how to organize the parts. Generally, you will not have unlimited time for giving an oral presentation, so you need to limit your focus to a few aspects of the topic that you can present effectively in the allotted time. After you have decided what the focus will be, it's helpful to think about the presentation's organization in terms of the beginning, the middle, and the end.

THE BEGINNING

The beginning or introduction of your presentation should do these three things:

1. Establish your credibility.
2. Interest the audience in the topic and make them want to listen.
3. Outline the main point and supporting points you will make.

Some experts estimate that you have about a minute to make a good first impression on your audience and engage their attention. An audience that is bored or confused by the introduction is likely to give less than full attention to the rest of the talk. And they may reject the message if the messenger doesn't seem credible. In the opening sentences, then, you must simultaneously orient the audience to the purpose and scope of your presentation and make them feel you are a trustworthy, credible speaker.

You establish your credibility, your *ethos*, by projecting good will towards the audience, revealing yourself as a person of good character, and being knowledgeable about your topic. You do this in part through nonverbal communication—through your dress, posture, facial expressions, and gestures—so it is important to make these work in your favor (more will be said about how to do so below under "Delivery"). But you can also establish credibility—as well as interest your audience—in the way you choose to introduce the topic. Here are some possibilities:

Begin with an anecdote that sets up a key issue you plan to discuss.
Because stories deal with concrete people, places, and events, they are more
memorable than abstract generalizations. They also get people's attention better than a dry statement such as, "In this presentation I will compare two ther-
apies for eating disorders." In a well-chosen anecdote you can illustrate a
problem or sketch quickly some key points of your presentation. Rather than
seeming artificial, the anecdote should lead naturally to a statement of the purpose of your talk and a brief overview of the body of the talk. If you have
engaged your audience's attention and shown your wisdom by framing your
message through an appropriate story, the audience will credit you with the
good sense and good character that wins their trust. And they will be prepared
to listen to the statement of your main point before you move to the body of
your speech.

Use brief, gentle humor. An audience perks up when a speaker opens
with something that everyone can laugh at. A joke or witty remark suggests to
them that you are relaxed and confident and that you do not want to bore them.
Humorous remarks must be related to the subject of your presentation, however, and must lead easily to a preview of its contents. Gratuitous, unrelated
humor might send the wrong message—that you are nervous, for example, or a
frustrated comedian, rather than someone to be taken seriously.

Say something startling or unexpected. The audience will likely know the
title or topic of your remarks ahead of time and will probably have some expectations of what you will say. You will generate greater interest if you begin with
a statement they *aren't* expecting. Offer a little-known statistic that points up
something unusual about your topic. Or make a seemingly implausible claim
that you'll support in the middle of your presentation. The audience will be
curious to see how you will make the startling statistic relevant or the unusual
claim plausible. Again, to win their trust, you must be prepared to move deftly
from this kind of opening to a statement of the key point of your message and
an overview of the facts, examples, or other evidence you will offer. You must
show you can say something significant, not merely shock your listeners.

Ask a rhetorical question. A rhetorical question is one that the speaker
does not expect anyone to answer out loud. But by asking the question and
pausing a moment while the audience members answer it silently in their own
minds, you are likely to gain everyone's involvement instantly. As you then proceed to outline and present your own answer to the question, you should have
the attention of your listeners. And if your answer differs from the one they
would have given, they will be particularly interested to learn why you think as
you do.

Give a brief demonstration. Like a story, a demonstration immediately provokes interest and helps to make the abstract concrete. It gives the audience something to watch as well as to hear, and therefore increases the chance they will remember your main point. Granted, it is easier and more appropriate to demonstrate some topics than others, so don't stretch imagination and credulity too thin. But if the presentation is about something that lends itself to a demonstration—for example, equipment, methods, or physical facts—consider a demonstration an excellent way to introduce your presentation. For example, suppose your speech was about the way smoking impairs health. To dramatize one health problem, the loss of lung capacity that smokers experience, you could have someone stand in front of the audience with nose and mouth taped shut, except for a small opening through which a drinking straw is inserted into the mouth. Have the person breathe through the straw for 30 seconds. As the person's face grows redder, the audience will see how difficult it is to get enough oxygen when the lungs can't be inflated fully.

Involve the audience in doing something. Most people learn better when they actually do something during a presentation rather than passively listen. If your audience is small enough, if you have some flexibility with the time allotted, and if your presentation is not supposed to be very formal, consider beginning by having one or more of your listeners do something: Ask a question and then call for volunteers to answer it. Involve a few members of the audience in a simple role play, game, or demonstration that illustrates one of your main points. Have everyone write for one minute about a topic that you give them; then have some of them share what they've written. Be aware, however, that the more you open your presentation up to audience participation, the less control you will have over it because someone may say or do something entirely unexpected or use up more of your precious time than you planned. If you choose this way of beginning, you need to plan carefully for all the eventualities you can think of; then you must be flexible and think quickly on your feet to recover from an unanticipated outcome. But if you are successful in involving the audience, you will earn not only their attention, but their respect and trust as well.

Whatever you choose as an attention-getter, be sure that you keep it relatively short in comparison to the rest of your talk. You can damage your credibility by being too funny or too enchanted by your method of getting attention or by taking so long to get to the point that people begin to wonder if you have one. Always follow your introduction with a clear and succinct statement of your main point and a quick overview of the middle of your presentation. It is usually a good idea to have some kind of visual aid that outlines your main point and the supporting points you intend to cover (visual aids will be discussed later in this chapter). Your audience will be able to listen for the key supporting points in the presentation if you outline them in advance.

THE MIDDLE

In the middle or body of your presentation, you elaborate on the points you previewed in your introduction. The number of points you should plan to cover depends on the time you have. In five minutes, you probably can do justice to only one; in fifteen minutes, only two or three. Even if you have been given 45-60 minutes to make your presentation, you would be wise not to elaborate on more than five points.

As you compose your presentation beforehand, think carefully about the best way to order the parts of your talk. For example, if your topic is historical, a chronological order might be the most appropriate. Or, for a topic that speculates on the future, it might be useful to discuss causes and then effects. But discussing effects first and causes second might be a good way to answer a question like "How did we get to the situation we're in now?"

Because your audience is listening to, not reading, your presentation, they won't have the benefit of headings, paragraph indentations, or boldfaced type to let them know what the main ideas are. You will need to draw their attention to the fact that you are stating a main point by saying something like, "My second point is. . . ." If you have created visual aids to supplement your speaking, you can use these to indicate that you are moving on to a new point.

You will need to give adequate illustrations, reasons, or other concrete data supporting each point. Because your audience can't re-read your text, repetitions and variations of supporting evidence will help them grasp the points more firmly. For example, you might give some statistics and then make an analogy showing the significance of these statistics in a more concrete context. Once again, visual aids are a big help with illustration of a point, particularly if a long quotation or numerical data are involved.

Avoid dwelling on a point too long, and don't assume that all of your points need the same emphasis. You might, for example, spend two minutes elaborating on a simple idea so that you can have ten minutes to spend on a more complex one. You should plan the relative amount of emphasis for each point ahead of time by carefully analyzing your audience's needs. Then you can adjust your emphasis during the presentation as you notice your audience's reaction. If they seem bored and fidgety, they are probably ready for you to move on. If they seem a bit confused or anxious, they may be hoping you will say something more to clarify the matter.

THE ENDING

Rather than assuming your conclusion will just take care of itself, or that you will simply stop talking when your time is up, you should plan the ending of your presentation as carefully as the beginning, The ending is the ideal time to reassert your main points, because research shows people remember beginnings and endings better than middles. If someone missed a point or two that you made in the middle, you can still hope to reach that person with an effective summary of your points.

Although summarizing is an important part of the conclusion, you can aim to do even more. In the conclusion you can relate the significance of your presentation to a broader context, perhaps even personalize the message for audience members so that they feel its significance more strongly. For example, if you have just spoken on the 1950-era McCarthy hearings in the US Senate, you could draw some comparisons between those events and current events of a similar nature. If the topic warrants it, at the end you can also issue a sort of challenge or call to action that inspires your listeners to do something with the information you have given them.

Whatever you do at the end of your presentation, provide a sense of closure that makes the audience feel they have come full circle with you in the minutes you've been talking. For example, you may allude to the anecdote, the joke, the rhetorical question, or the demonstration you began with. Say something to help the audience understand how the expectations you aroused with your introduction have now been fulfilled. In that way, they will sense that you have given the topic a full and satisfying treatment and not simply run out of time.

USING RESOURCES WISELY

Because there are important differences between listening to and reading a text, you should consider these differences as you prepare an oral presentation. Unlike written words, which are more or less permanent, spoken words vanish almost immediately. While readers can pause and reread parts of a text that aren't clear at first, in a formal setting listeners usually don't have the luxury of interrupting and asking the speaker to repeat things. As you understand the differences between writing and speaking, you can prepare to capitalize on the advantages of face-to-face communication as well as compensate for the transitory nature of speech. In planning your presentation, you should consider each of three resources that can enhance your oral message if used properly—or detract from it if you fail to take them into account. These resources are time, the environment for your talk, and visual aids.

TIME

In most cases, you will be told early on that you can speak a specific number of minutes. (If you are not told, be sure to ask how much time you'll have.) But be aware that the amount of time you are promised and what you may actually get are often not the same. For example, at meetings of professional organizations, you may be one member of a panel of three or four speakers, each of whom is supposed to talk for 20 minutes. But if you are the last speaker and the speaker just before you takes 30 minutes, you may be forced to cut your presentation. Or if one of the speakers fails to show up, you may suddenly have the dubious luxury of speaking ten minutes longer than planned. Because of unexpected events like these, you should plan in advance where you could condense or expand your presentation if you had to. Rather than adding another point or extra detail to your talk, one good way of using additional time is to ask for questions and comments from the audience. Try to anticipate how the audience might react to your presentation so you can be prepared with good responses.

PLANNING FOR DELIVERY

Once you have analyzed your rhetorical situation, organized your presentation, and considered how to use the resources available, you are ready to prepare for the moment of truth—the time when you actually deliver your message.

Delivery is the most important part of an oral presentation. Even if you have prepared thoroughly, all of your hard work may come to naught if you can't deliver your message effectively. To be successful you should consider how presenting a message orally differs from giving a reader a written text. As a speaker, you can capitalize on important differences in these two types of rhetorical situations. In the oral situation, listeners have the advantage of hearing your actual voice and watching you deliver your message. You can use your voice, appearance, personal traits, gestures and body language to enhance the reception of your message in a way that you can't when you write. Planning and practicing your delivery involves the following: (1) deciding what method of memory support to use, (2) choosing appropriate dress and grooming, and (3) rehearsing to make your voice and body movements support your message.

MEMORY SUPPORT

Although you may occasionally be called on without warning to give an impromptu speech, usually you are given time to prepare. As you look ahead to the time when you will speak, you should decide whether you will speak from memory, from notes, or from a complete manuscript. Memorizing your presentation is good mental discipline; it can also make you so familiar with your material that you feel more confident and poised. For some people, however, memorizing a speech can lead to a colorless, rote presentation and inflexibility in adapting to the occasion and the audience. Others may freeze if their minds suddenly go blank and they aren't able to improvise with words other than the ones they memorized. Because of these potential pitfalls, memorizing an entire presentation is usually not the best option.

Speaking from notes is probably far more common in today's academic and professional world than is speaking from memory. Using notes permits you to sound natural and to maintain good eye contact; it may also make you feel free to move about naturally. Your notes might take the form of a simple one-page outline of your presentation that you can set in front of you and glance at, or some 3x5 cards on which you have written key words and which you can hold discreetly in one hand. Focusing your mind on concepts and key words rather than entire sentences allows you to speak extemporaneously, using the words that seem appropriate for the purpose and audience. If you are interrupted while speaking extemporaneously from notes, you can recover easily, without having to worry about exact wording. If you prepare a computer presentation, a handout, or transparencies, these often take the place of notes, as you simply need to look at what you have written on your visual aids to prompt you in your speaking.

For more formal occasions, reading from a prepared manuscript may be the best option, particularly if the audience is large and you will have to remain at a lectern with a microphone. Reading from a text is also helpful if you are trying to communicate something delicate, and you have worked very carefully beforehand to find just the right words for your message. Also, if you want to create a certain mood and images with your words, you may want to read from a prepared manuscript. Reading from a manuscript is often the manner of delivery used at professional conferences where social scientists share their research findings. The scripts of their oral presentations may become the basis for eventual publications.

Reading your speech doesn't have to be monotonous and boring if you practice your delivery enough times that you can say your sentences effectively while still looking up frequently to maintain eye contact with the audience. To facilitate finding your place again easily after you look up, prepare your manuscript in a large font with wide margins and triple spacing. Don't feel so tied to what you have written that you don't feel comfortable improvising a little—tossing off a spontaneous comment related to the occasion or pausing to offer a simple explanation for something your audience seems puzzled about.

APPROPRIATE DRESS

Dressing and grooming yourself appropriately on the day of your presentation can't be overemphasized. People form first impressions about you based on your appearance, and, as unfair as it may seem, if they form negative impressions, your audience will probably not be able to judge the merits of your presentation objectively. Even though you may view your clothing, hairstyle, and jewelry as your way of making a statement about your personality, putting your individuality as your first priority can distract or even alienate your audience. Celebrities may be able to get away with eccentric dress, unusual hairstyles, and excessive jewelry, but because you are trying to establish your credibility, you would be wise to conform to the style that others follow in a given setting.

You should not dress less formally than your audience because your prominence as the speaker will make your casual clothing even more conspicuous than it would otherwise be. On the other hand, if you are dressed up a bit more than the audience, they may take it as a compliment to them; they certainly won't judge you as being careless about your dress. Often, you can adjust your clothing in simple ways to fit in. If the other men in the audience are all tieless and in shirtsleeves, for example, a man may be able to remove his jacket and tie to be like them. Women can also remove accessories to achieve a more relaxed, understated look and blend in with how other women in the audience are dressed. If you are unsure about what to wear, ask ahead of time.

VOICE QUALITIES

Just as you want your appearance to enhance your delivery, you need to consider how you can use your voice to have the right impact on your audience. The first thing to consider is the *volume*, or loudness, of your voice. If you will be speaking into a microphone, you will merely need to be sure that you are close enough to it and that it is amplifying your voice adequately for everyone in the room. When there is no microphone, you need to speak loudly enough for people in the rear to hear you without straining. If you have a naturally quiet voice, you will need to make a conscious effort to project your voice more than usual. You can practice by rehearsing your speech for a friend in a room the size of the one you'll be speaking in.

You also need to consider the *pitch*, or high and low tones, of your voice. Interesting speakers vary their pitch rather than droning on at the same level all the time. Lowering the pitch of your voice can add a sense of drama and solemnity to what you say, while raising it can impart a sense of urgency.

The *pace* of your delivery is also important for achieving the effect you want to have on your audience. Pace is simply the speed you speak at. Most speakers average between 125 and 150 words per minute. At this rate, it takes you about two minutes to read a standard page of typewritten text. You can slow your pace down to emphasize points or to discuss complex ideas, or you can speed it up a bit to show excitement or cover some simple ideas quickly. Talking too slow or too fast all the time, however, will make it difficult for your audience to listen: Their minds will start to wander if you are too slow, and they will become confused and frustrated if you race through your presentation faster than they can comprehend it.

Finally, you must take care to articulate your words clearly, pronouncing them according to common standards, and to use correct grammar. Articulating "did you eat yet?" as "jeetyet?" may be acceptable in a conversation with friends, but it will convey excessive casualness in a presentation to an audience. Similarly, if you pronounce "exactly" as "ezackly," your audience may believe you are not well educated. Likewise, making grammatical errors such as "He done it" or "Me and him went" will seriously detract from your credibility. As with your dress and grooming, you risk conveying the wrong impression if you insist on using idiosyncratic speech or a dialect that is considered non-standard.

NONVERBAL COMMUNICATION

Although using your voice carefully can help make your delivery memorable, equally important are the nonverbal ways you communicate your message. A key factor here is eye contact. Speakers who seldom look into the eyes of their audience members convey the impression of being painfully shy and nervous or, perhaps worse, indifferent to the audience. On the other hand, a speaker who makes frequent eye contact with individuals in the audience reassures them that he or she is poised and prepared, keeps their attention, can assess how they are receiving the message, and can make subtle corrections as needed. Making eye contact means that you actually look into the eyes of different people in different parts of the room. You should hold one person's gaze for 3–5 seconds before moving on to someone else.

Gestures are another form of nonverbal communication that can enhance or detract from a message. Gestures are movements, both voluntary and involuntary, that can illustrate or emphasize a point, such as striking the podium with your fist to demonstrate your determination. (Admittedly, this particular gesture may be overdramatic, and it is certainly not one to use often.) Many people gesture naturally, using their fingers to point or to enumerate, or spreading their hands to indicate size. Others find it difficult to "talk with their hands." Too much gesturing may make you seem a bit frantic and distract your audience; too little gesturing may make you seem wooden and unnatural. As you rehearse your presentation, have a friend pay attention to your natural gestures; then make a conscious effort to eliminate distracting ones and to make the remaining ones smooth and effective. If you don't make many gestures naturally, think of appropriate ones you could make and practice them until they become natural. It is important to have some animated gestures during your presentation because they will help keep your audience alert and involved.

Your other movements, posture, and facial expressions also communicate your attitude and emotional state to your audience. Even though you may feel butterflies in your stomach, if your talk is well-focused and organized, there's really nothing to dread. Move confidently to the position you will occupy as speaker. If you will be standing, keep your feet about 10–12 inches apart, relax your knees, then keep them slightly bent. Take a deep breath and let your shoulders drop naturally rather than keeping them hunched up around your neck. Pause a moment to survey your audience and smile at them. If you are not tied by necessity to a lectern, move about a little in front of your audience, but avoid pacing. Channeling your nervousness into appropriate movements as you speak will help dissipate your anxiety and will make you seem animated and at ease.

REHEARSING YOUR DELIVERY

Just as actors and singers rehearse before performing, good speakers do too. You need to practice integrating all the things you've learned in this chapter, and make your presentation a seamless whole. The better rehearsed your presentation is, the more confident you will feel and the more poised you will appear to your audience. If you practice using your visual aids, you will be able to control them and any necessary equipment smoothly, without unduly interrupting your talk and losing audience attention. Finally, if you rehearse your presentation several times you will be able to judge how well your presentation fits into the time limits you've been given and be more able to adjust its length as needed.

Asking a friend to listen to you and watch you has already been mentioned as one effective rehearsal strategy. Be sure to ask a friend who will be honest with you and critical enough of your performance to offer helpful feedback rather than simply reassure you that you're doing fine. Another rehearsal method is to practice in front of a full-length mirror. Still another is to have someone videotape you as you give a dress rehearsal; then watch the videotape several times to see where you can improve your performance.

Though all of these preparations may seem extensive and elaborate for just a few minutes on stage, after you successfully deliver your first oral presentations, you will find that you can prepare more quickly and easily for succeeding ones. Following many of the steps detailed here will become second nature, and you will become a more confident and polished public speaker.

INDEX

Page numbers followed by f indicate a figure
Page numbers followed by t indicate a table